BIRDS OF ESSEX COUNTY, NEW YORK

by

Geoffrey Carleton

Edited by John M.C. Peterson

Published by

High Peaks Audubon Society, Inc.
Elizabethtown, New York

Third Edition
1999

ACKNOWLEDGEMENT

The author wishes to thank John M.C. Peterson

*For all his help in getting this book
through the press.*

*Thanks also to Richard W. MacDonald
and John G. Thaxton
for their skilled and tireless production support.*

G.C.

Printed in the United States of America
Third Edition

Library of Congress Catalog Card Number: 99-72086

ISBN 0-9668819-1-5

ISO 9706
This paper meets the die requirements of ISO
9706:1994, Information and documentation – Paper
for documents – Requirements for performance.

Printed by
Thomson-Shore, Inc.
Dexter, Michigan

FOREWORD

High Peaks Audubon is honored to present this completely revised Third Edition of *Birds of Essex County, New York*, by Geoffrey Carleton. For over 70 years, Carleton made a study of the birds of the Adirondack-Champlain region. This work is the product of that prodigious study, with avian data compiled from a search of the literature (back to the 18th and 19th centuries), examination of local bird and egg collections, and the reports of numerous observers.

Essex County, New York, includes both the High Peaks region of Adirondacks and the lowlands of the Champlain Valley. The county holds the highest mountains in the state – Marcy (elev. 5344') – and borders the sixth largest lake in the United States – Champlain (95' above sea level). With an area of 1,097 square miles and a population of about 35,000, the county is nearly the size of Delaware, but with only about 5 percent of the population of that state. All of Essex County lies within the boundaries of the Adirondack Park.

Founded in 1973, High Peaks Audubon Society, Inc., is one of about 500 chapters of the National Audubon Society. The chapter represents all of Essex County. Monthly meetings feature special speakers, films, and slides. Field trips are conducted throughout the region by noted experts. Members receive the bimonthly, full-color *AUDUBON* magazine, plus the bimonthly *High Peaks Audubon Newsletter*. The chapter takes an active role in environmental matters, especially in the Adirondack-Champlain region.

Further information regarding membership and chapter activities is available upon request from High Peaks Audubon Society, Inc., Discovery Farm, RR 1, Box 230, Elizabethtown, NY 12932-9721.

Mary Buehler
President

Keene, NY
April, 1999

PATRONS

Dr. Kenneth B. Adams

In Memory of Alice Bonk & Eileen Buehler

The Buehler family

Chappy & Cathy Chapman

Glen & Malinda Bergamini Chapman and family

Joan Clark,
In Memory of Dewey

Charlcie Delehanty

Bob & Jackie Hagar

Michael L. Hough

Gordon E. Howard

Keene Garden Center, Inc.

Dr. and Mrs. Wesley E. Lanyon

Richard W. Lawrence, Jr.

Richard W. MacDonald

Richard Steven Marrus, M.D.

The Mountaineer

National Audubon Society of New York State

Jane Ann Owens

John M.C. & Susan French Peterson

Nancy B. Pierce

In Memory of Winifred Notman Prince

Dave & Kathy Rutkowski

Dean T. Spaulding

John & Patricia Thaxton

Dr. Donald J. & Janice E. Timmons

Susan & Bob Wei

Birds of Essex County, New York

Third edition, through April 30, 1999
by
Geoffrey Carleton

310 species are listed, of which 190 breed or have bred. A scale of abundance has been devised suggesting numbers an active observer might see in a season, its value perhaps more relative than absolute:

Abundant .... over 200
Common 50-200
Fairly Common 20-50
Uncommon 5-20
Rare 1-5
Very Rare .... Every several years

Abbreviations

Atlas – 1980-85 NYS Breeding Bird Atlas Project
CBC – Christmas Bird Count
DEC – NYS Department of Environmental Conservation
E'town – Elizabethtown
HiPkAu – High Peaks Audubon Society
imm - immature
NYSARC – NYS Avian Records Committee
pr – permanent resident
sr – summer resident
SUNY – State U. at Plattsburgh
sv – summer visitant
Ti – Ticonderoga
tv – transient visitant
wv – winter visitant

Nomenclature follows current usage in *field notes* and the sequence of species of the A.O.U.'s *Check-list of North American Birds, Seventh Edition*, 1998, used in *field notes*.

Photo front cover Warren Greene
Map Richard W. MacDonald

Initialed Observers

EA	—	Elizabeth Anderson	RG	—	Richard P. Guthrie
BB	—	Bartlett Bailey	GH	—	Gordon E. Howard
DB	—	Dirck Benson	JH	—	Joseph Hart
IB	—	Isabelle H. Bailey	RH	—	Robert K. Hagar
JB	—	Jean Beck	TH	—	George "Terry" Hall
JBB	—	John B. Brown	SI	—	Selma Isil
JDB	—	John D. Bruce	CEJ	—	Charles E. Johnson
MAB	—	Mary A. Buehler			(see Bibliography)
MB	—	Merry E. Baker	EJ	—	Elsbeth S. Johnson
MKB	—	Mary K. Benson	AK	—	Allen E. Kemnitzer
NB	—	Nicholas B. Bailey	JK	—	Joseph Keji
RB	—	Ray Bender	MK	—	Marguerite Kingsbury
RBB	—	Russell B. Bailey	MJK	—	Marshall J. Kinne
TB	—	Thomas C. Barber	CL	—	Charlotte Ladwig
WB	—	William T. Brown	GL	—	Gary Lee
AC	—	Ann M. Chapman	RL	—	Robert Ladwig
BC	—	Bernard Carman	RBL	—	Richard B. LaVallee
DC	—	Dewey Clark	RWL	—	Richard W. Lawrence, Jr.
DLC	—	Dean L. Cook	TL	—	Thomas A. Lesperance
GC	—	Geoffrey Carleton	WL	—	Wesley E. Lanyon
GDC	—	Glen D. Chapman	BM	—	Betsy MacMillan
GTC	—	Greenleaf T. Chase	DM	—	Derek Moore
JAC	—	Joan A. Clark	EAM	—	Esther Ann MacCready
JC	—	Janet Cooper	EBM	—	Elizabeth B. McNulty
TC	—	Thomas Carrolan	GM	—	Gordon M. Meade
WC	—	Walter M. Chapman	JM	—	John MacMillan
WAC	—	William A. Casselman	KM	—	Keith C. Murphy
HD	—	Harriet L. Delafield	LM	—	Lawrence L. Master
TD	—	Thomas Dudones	MM	—	Marion Mason
BE	—	Beth Edmonds	MAM	—	Mark A. Manske
EE	—	Elon H. Eaton (see	NM	—	Nancy Master
		Bibliography)	NLM	—	Nancy L. Martin
WE	—	Walter G. Ellison	PM	—	Paul Matray
DF	—	Darrell Ford	RM	—	Ruth Miller
GF	—	Greg Furness	RWM	—	Richard W. MacDonald
AG	—	August Gabel	SM	—	Scott Morrical
DG	—	Deborah A. Goslin	TM	—	Theodore D. Mack
EG	—	Edward C. Grant, Jr.	TNM	—	T. Norman Mason
MG	—	Mark Gretch	DN	—	Daniel W. Nickerson

AO	—	Antoinette O'Bryan	MS	—	Mary Sheffield
KO	—	Kathryn O'Keeffe	MLS	—	Marion L. Smith
LO	—	Lydia Osenbaugh	NS	—	Nina Schoch
NO	—	Nancy L. Olsen	PS	—	Phebe Sweatt
PO	—	Paul Osenbaugh	RS	—	Robert Sheffield
SO	—	Sean O'Brien	RSt	—	Rudolph Stone
AP	—	Alan Pistorius	TS	—	Trisha J. Spaulding
AGP	—	Augustus G. Paine	WS	—	Wayne Scott
JP	—	John M.C. Peterson	WRS	—	Walter R. Spofford
JPa	—	John Parke	DT	—	Donald J. Timmons, Jr.
NP	—	Nat Parke	JT	—	Joseph W. Taylor
SP	—	Susan French Peterson	JGT	—	John G. Thaxton
WP	—	William A.B. Peterson	JET	—	Janice E. Timmons
DR	—	David M. Rutkowski	PT	—	Particia A. Taber
AR	—	Atea Ring	PHT	—	Patricia H. Thaxton
GR	—	Gary A. Randorf	ST	—	Susan Turner
GBR	—	Gerald B. Rosenband	MV	—	Margaret Vetter
HR	—	Hallam Ring	CW	—	Cecelia Wojciukiewicz
AAS	—	Aretas A. Saunders	DW	—	Dennis Wells
		(see Bibliography)	FW	—	Frederick A.C.
ASt	—	Anne Straight			Wardenburg III
CS	—	Carole A. Slatkin	GW	—	George Williams
DS	—	David Schwarz	HW	—	Hollis White
DTS	—	Dean T. Spaulding	MW	—	M.L. Ward
FRS	—	Frank R. Schetty	RW	—	Robert C. Wei
LRS	—	Langdon R. Stevenson	WW	—	William Watson
LS	—	Linwood Sherman	DY	—	David Young

How to use this Book

In addition to the list of 310 species recorded in Essex County, this book provides concise information on rarity, seasonality, abundance, and other history for each bird. All records are documented by place, date, and observer. An examination of the first species, **Red-throated Loon**, may help readers understand subsequent entries:

> Rare tv. Crown Point April 9, 1994 (JP, DS, RM) to
> Crown Point May 11, 1985 (TB, JP); Crown Point October
> 25, 1986 (WE) to Westport December 28, 1998 (JP, DTS).
> Max. 20 Port Kent November 8, 1992 (JBB, TM).

"Rare" suggests that an active observer might see one to five in a season. A transient visitant ("tv.") occurs only in migration. Red-throated Loons winter mainly at sea, along the east coast from Newfoundland to the Gulf of Mexico; the closest breeding grounds are near the mouth of the St. Lawrence River. Heading north to Canada in spring, they pass through Essex County between the extreme dates of April 9-May 11. After nesting, they return to the county in the fall and may linger into winter, from October 25-December 28; usually solitary, the most seen at one time were 20 at Port Kent on November 8. Notice that the places, dates, and observers serve to document these records. The locations (Crown Point, Port Kent, and Westport) also suggest that most Red-throated Loons are found along Lake Champlain, with Crown Point a favored spot.

A comparison with the next entry shows that the **Common Loon** arrives earlier (March 2), stays later (into January), is sometimes more abundant in passage, and can be found nesting on county lakes and ponds.

For further information on the birds in this book, please consult the Bibliography or any of the popular field guides. New records are published quarterly in *The Kingbird*. Good birding!

John M.C. Peterson, Editor

SPECIES ACCOUNTS

Red-throated Loon
Rare tv. Crown Point April 9, 1994 (JP, DS, RWM) to Crown Point May 11, 1985 (TB, JP); Crown Point October 25, 1986 (WE) to Westport December 28, 1998 (JP, DTS). Max. 20 Port Kent November 8, 1992 (JBB, TM).

Common Loon
Rare sr, fairly common tv. Whallon's Bay March 2, 1997 (RWM, JP, SP, DTS) to Westport January 2, 1971 (MLS) and January 28, 1975 (TB). Fall arrival Whallon's Bay September 18, 1978 (JP). The 1984-85 Adirondack Loon Survey found breeding pairs on 13 lakes and ponds, with chicks seen on seven: Arbutus, Boreas, McKenzie, and Mink Ponds, and Catlin, Rich, and Third [Essex Chain] Lakes (DEC). In 1998, the NY Loon Conservation Project found pairs on 16 lakes and ponds, with chicks seen on nine: Big, Johnson, McKenzie, New, Putnam, Stony, and Wolf Ponds, and Pharaoh and Pyramid Lakes (Audubon Soc. Of NYS). Non-breeding birds occur on Lake Champlain in early summer. Max. c. 100 Willsboro Bay October 31, 1976 (*fide* PS); Whallon's Bay all summer 1980 (JPa).

Pied-billed Grebe
Rare sr. Whallon's Bay March 22, 1975 (GC, Irene A. Carleton) to Westport November 29, 1976 (PT); Westport January 4, 1976 (GC) and January 4, 1997 (RWM, JP, DTS); Essex January 9, 1977 (JP). Max. six Webb Royce Swamp July 11, 1992 (TM, JP).

Horned Grebe
Common tv, occasional in winter. Heart Bay September 3, 1983 (DC) to Essex May 28, 1974 (JP). Max. 38 Whallon's Bay December 6, 1997 (TM).

Red-necked Grebe
Uncommon tv. Ray Brook April 4, 1986 (EG) to Moriah May 16, 1967 (TNM); Mirror Lake August 13, 1978 (NM, LM); Westport October 18, 1972 (GC) to Westport December 18, 1976 (Ferrisburg CBC) and Essex February 22, 1995 (RWM). Max. 32 Port Henry April 18, 1996 (RWM, JP). Fall max. seven Lake Placid November 1, 1992 (RH, TM).

Eared Grebe
 Westport December 18, 1976 (DG, PT).

Yellow-nosed Albatross
 Crown Point May 8, 1994 (JP, DTS); accepted by NYSARC as *Diomedea*, sp. [now *Thalassarche* sp.].

Northern Fulmar
 Lake Placid December 2, 1995 (Sentinel Rd. – David Brant); rehabilitated and transferred December 11 to Massachusetts for coastal release.

American White Pelican
 October 15, 1862 (EE).

Double-crested Cormorant
 Fairly common sr, rare in winter. Has bred at Four Brothers since 1984 (max. 1,394 nests 1998, RWM). Port Henry April 4, 1998 (RWM, JP) to Willsboro Bay January 12, 1997 (RWM, JP, MAB, DTS); Mirror Lake August 29-31, 1984 (NM). 1,250 Four Brothers July 29, 1994 (RWM, JP).

American Bittern
 Uncommon sr. Saranac River March 21, 1964 (JH) to Saranac River November 6, 1972 (RH).

Least Bittern
 Bulwagga Bay May 2, 1988 (EJ); two pairs at Ti marsh in the 1930s, latest August 29, 1935 (GC); present in 1975 (BM, GC) and May 17, 1980 (EJ, JP, DT, JET). Wickham Marsh July 9, 1976 (Dr. Harold G. Klein and Ecology class).

Great Blue Heron
 Uncommon tv and sr. Crown Point March 17, 1985 (JDB) to Ti January 22, 1977 (*fide* BM) and Willsboro Point February 15, 1983 (RM); has bred at Four Brothers since 1993 (max. 27 nests 1996, RWM, JP); 21 nests Webb Royce Swamp April 15, 1995 (JP); 40 nests Hoffman Road beaver pond, Schroon, July 27, 1998 (Evelyn Greene).

Great Egret
 Very rare sv and tv. Bulwagga Bay May 14, 1990 (GH, KM, JP); Keene July 5, 1998 (ST); Westport July 24, 1991 (GC) to Crown Point

September 17, 1993 (GF). Max: three Webb Royce Swamp August 6, 1997 (NO, JP, DTS). There were sightings at Barber Pond in 1948, 1992, 1994, and 1997.

Snowy Egret
Westport May 8, 1984 (GC); two Four Brothers June 19 and 26, 1976 (JP, WP *et al.*); one Four Brothers August 23 1985 (LS).

Tricolored Heron
Westport May 26, 1989 (GC, TNM); Crown Point August 15, 1983 (GC, RH).

Cattle Egret
Has bred at Four Brothers since 1973 (max. 20 nests 1974 – Elvin Cross, Jr., JP); St. Armand May 2, 1976 (GTC, RH); Essex July, 11-22, 1974 (JP, GC); Willsboro summer 1974 (JPa); Crown Point early August 1962 (MLS); Ray Brook August 30, 1994 (Sue Capone); Westport October 20, 1995 (Robert Turck); two Whallonsburg October 24, 1991 (KM, JP); Reber November 10-12, 1983 (Eugene and Friend Cross).

Green Heron
Uncommon sr in lowlands. Westport April 26, 1979 (JET) to Ray Brook October 6, 1966 (JK) and Westport October 6, 1988 (GC).

Black-crowned Night-Heron
Breeds Four Brothers: Normand St. Jacques found 90 nests in 1954, DEC 89 in 1979, HiPkAu max. 171 in 1997. Bred Schuyler Is. in 1955 (TL) and Webb Royce Swamp in 1989 (JPa, NP). Otherwise uncommon sv. Westport April 9, 1997 (TB, JP) to Four Brothers September 12, 1998 (RWM).

Dean T. Spaulding

Black-crowned Night-Heron, Four Brothers

Glossy Ibis
Two Bulwagga Bay May 15, 1990 (Ruth Kufahl, GL, KM, JP); one flying from Shelburne Farms, Vermont, to apparent roost Four Brothers May 24, 1997 (SM, Ted Murin).

Turkey Vulture
Casual before 1969, now a fairly common tv and sr. Chilson March 18, 1995 (DR) to Wadhams November 8, 1978 (EAM, JP); Blue Ridge Road January 8, 1996 (TD). An unusual location was Lake Placid July 3, 1975 (JT). Max. 28 Westport August 1975 (HR).

Greater White-fronted Goose
Westport November 18, 1996 (RWM, DTS).

Snow Goose
Uncommon tv. North Hudson March 5, 1992 (William Endicott) to Crown Point May 28, 1995 (JP); Four Brothers June 10, 1987 (JP), June 16, 1978 (Robert Yunick), and August 2, 1996 (RWM); Coot Hill October 3, 1978 (EAM, JP) to Whallon's Bay January 25, 1982 (JDB). Max. 4,000 Essex December 5, 1998 (JP, JGT, PHT).

> Blue morphs Crown Point April 9, 1984 (GF) to Coot Hill April 19, 1989 (EJ); Crown Point October 28, 1989 (GF) to Westport December 17, 1988 (TM, KM, JP).

Canada Goose
Abundant tv; there are now dates throughout the year. Has nested at Four Brothers since 1973; five goslings Webb Royce Swamp May 15, 1995 (MG); on nest Essex Station April 22, 1997 (JP, DTS). Max. 100,000 Essex November 5, 1977 (George Tart *et al.*); 22 small individuals Whallon's Bay March 5 and 6, 1976 (JP, PT); one small form Whallon's Bay December 5, 1998 (SO, TM, JP, JGT, PHT).

Brant
Very rare tv. Santanoni Preserve May 14, 1978 (WC) to Ray Brook June 2, 1996 (TD); Four Brothers June 9, 1954 (W.R. Miller), June 15, 1991 (GL), June 22, 1995 (RWM, DTS), and June 23, 1980 (JP); Essex July 13, 1969 (FW); Essex October 10, 1980 (JPa) to Mirror Lake November 11-16, 1997 (RWM, NS); Lake Flower most of winter 1979-80 (TM). Max. 300+ Crown Point May 20, 1996 (DM).

Mute Swan
Apparently feral bird appeared Ray Brook October 29, 1953; was shot

by hunter (*fide* GM, *Kingbird* 3:75).

Tundra Swan
 Crown Point March 1933 (GW); northbound migrant Lake George March 11, 1991 (Dan Spada); Scarface Mt. November 18, 1972 (TM); three Crown Point November 29-December 3, 1982, then Bulwagga Bay December 4 (Mr. & Mrs. Hughes Kilburn).

Wood Duck
 Fairly common sr. Wilmington March 15, 1990 (RH) to Westport November 18, 1974 (GC). Four winter records. Max. 75 Ti September 8, 1971 (GTC).

Gadwall
 April 1882 (EE); Essex April 3, 1997 (TB, JP) to Westport January 17, 1999 (JP, DTS). Has bred Four Brothers since 1977 (GC, JP); two nests June 8, 1996 (JP). Max. 15 Four Brothers June 10, 1991 (LRS).

American Wigeon
 Very rare tv. Essex March 13, 1975 (JP) to Essex April 9, 1974 (JP); pair Webb Royce Swamp March 28, 1998 (MG); two drakes Coll Bay April 9, 1999 (JP, JGT, PHT); Webb Royce Swamp April 16, 1997 (TB, JP)-April 22, 1997 (JP, DTS); pair Webb Royce Swamp April 22, 1995 (JP) and May 20, 1995 (MG), one there July 11, 1992 (TM, JP). Westport October 13, 1970 (GC); Crown Point October 22, 1937 (GW); Westport December 20, 1997 (KM, PHT *et al.*); Lake Placid December 27, 1998 (LM) and December 28, 1997 (unusual inland — LM); Whallon's Bay December 30-31, 1976 (GBR, CS); Westport January 9, 1979 (JP, GBR).

American Black Duck
 Uncommon sr, common wv. Max. 5,000 Whallon's Bay April 16, 1976 (JP, WP).

Mallard
 Uncommon tv, rare wv. Numbers at Essex as late as May 19, 1979 (JP, RBB). Max. 1,000 North West Bay February 15, 1999 (JGT, PHT); 35 nests Four Brothers May 13, 1992 (David Capen). Feral birds present throughout the year. Hybrids with American Black Duck are rare, but regular.

Blue-winged Teal
Uncommon tv, rare sr. Essex April 7, 1974 (JP) to Ti November 5, 1975 (BM). Max. 30 Westport August 26, 1978 (EAM, JP). Breeds at Essex Station.

Northern Shoveler
Whallon's Bay March 16, 1985 (CW); four Westport April 9, 1999 (WW); two pairs Moody Pond April 17, 1995 (RH); three males E'town April 18, 1978 (JP); male Webb Royce Swamp April 26, 1997 (MG); Saranac River May 24, 1965 (HD, JH); possible breeder (Atlas). October 7, 1885 (EE); five Westport December 13, 1984 (EJ, JP).

Northern Pintail
Rare tv. and wv. Westport December 10, 1977 (GC, Mike DiNunzio, PT) to Webb Royce Swamp May 1, 1995 (MG); possible breeder (Atlas). Hen Westport September 14, 1987 (GC); Whallon's Bay September 17, 1979 (GBR, CS); Crown Point October 25, 1989 (GF). Max. 20 Westport February 20, 1999 (MG).

Green-winged Teal
Rare tv and very rare sr. Essex March 27, 1976 (HiPkAu) to Whallonsburg May 11, 1979 (RBB, JP); Ti August 20, 1946 (GC) to Crown Point October 27, 1937 (GC) and Webb Royce Swamp November 22, 1998 (TM, SO). Westport December 19, 1998 (TM, RW). Drakes at Essex July 2, 1974 (GBR, CS), two Essex Station June 11, 1977 (GC) and Ray Pond June 9, 1972 (GC); six Webb Royce Swamp July 10, 1993 (JBB, TM), hen there August 6, 1995 (JP, DTS, JGT, PHT). Confirmed breeder (Atlas). Max. 20 Whallonsburg April 16, 1997 (TB, JP).

Canvasback
Usually rare tv and wv. Heart Bay October 11, 1981 (DLC) to Ti April 10, 1969 (JC). Max. 1,800 Willsboro and Port Kent January 10, 1976 (JP *et al.*).

Redhead
Rare tv and wv. Three Westport October 18-30, 1975 (GC, TNM, JP, PT) to drake off Wickham Marsh March 5, 1983 (MG); Essex Station May 14, 1977 (GR *et al.*). Max. six Westport January 17, 1999 (JP, DTS)

Ring-necked Duck

Uncommon wv. Hadley Pond September 27, 1997 (RWM, JP) to
Westport May 4, 1979 (PT). Bred Port Douglas 1955 (TL); has bred
Cherry Patch Pond (TM); pair Webb Royce Swamp April 22, 1995 (JP)
and three pair May 1, 1995 (MG). Max. 140 Moody Pond November
7, 1993 (RH).

Greater Scaup

Uncommon wv. Westport September 19, 1979 (GBR, CS) to Crown
Point May 24, 1996 (DN, RW). Pair Four Brothers July 21, 1994
(LRS).

Lesser Scaup

Rare tv. Whallon's Bay March 16, 1985 (Peter Capainola, Robert
Dickerman, JP) to Schroon Lake May 11, 1974 (JB) and Crown Point
May 11, 1996 (JP, RW). Heart Bay October 2, 1977 (DLC) to
Westport November 24, 1974 (GC). Westport January 24, 1998
(RWM). Max. 27 Schroon Lake November 7, 1975 (JB).

King Eider

Lake Champlain, Essex Co. December 2, 1894 (EE — specimen in
State Museum at Albany); imm. drake Crown Point December 23, 1993
(TH, SM, Ruth Reames — accepted VT Records Committee).

Harlequin Duck

Imm. drake Essex January 12-22, 1986 (TM, JP, *et al.*).

Surf Scoter

Rare wv. Pair Essex May 2, 1994 (ASt, Carlos Straight); Heart Bay
September 24, 1977 (DLC) to Westport January 12, 1975 (JP, PT).
Max. 15 Lake Placid October 16, 1965 (JT).

White-winged Scoter

Uncommon tv and wv. Lincoln Pond April 19, 1976 (DN) to Heart
Bay May 24, 1991 (DLC); pair Four Brothers June 11, 1988 (NB, GL,
JP); Four Brothers June 12, 1993 (GL, RWM, JP, DTS); Four Brothers
June 19, 1989 (NB, JP, SP); Heart Bay September 24, 1977 (DC) to
Essex January 27, 1974 (JP). Max. 25 Mirror Lake November 3, 1988
(RH) and Crown Point May 24, 1996 (DN, JP, RW).

Black Scoter

Rare tv and wv. Westport April 6, 1997 (TB, JP) to Essex May 10, 1966 (FW); Heart Bay September 24, 1977 (DLC) to Westport January 31, 1975 (TB, TNM). Max. 170 Mirror Lake November 3, 1988 (RH, CL, RL).

Oldsquaw

Uncommon tv and wv. Crown Point April 6, 1997 (TB, RWM, JP) to Lake Placid May 30, 1970 (JT); Lake Placid October 17, 1965 (JT) to Essex January 24, 1974 (JP).

Bufflehead

Fairly common tv and wv. Hadley Pond October 16, 1979 (KM, JP) to Westport May 22, 1976 (DG, JP, PT). Two Boreas River near Tahawus early June 1976 (TM). Max. 150 Willsboro Point November 22, 1977 (GC).

Common Goldeneye

Abundant tv. Winters where there is open water. Westport October 6, 1988 (GC) to Ti May 19, 1979 (Lowell Martin) and Crown Point May 19, 1991 (JP). Very rare sr. Hen with brood Willsboro Point May 1, 1995 (MG) and off Wickham Marsh July 17, 1997 (JP). Sv Four Brothers August 29-31, 1986 (RBB, TM, JP) and Whallon's Bay September 11, 1975 (JP). Max. 1,100 Port Kent January 17, 1998 (JP, JGT, PHT).

Barrow's Goldeneye

Rare wv. Drake Whallon's Bay November 16, 1990 (GC, RH) to drake Westport April 22, 1983 (GC, TNM, JP). Pair off Wickham Marsh January 29, 1995 (JP, DTS); pair Crown Point March 23, 1989 (GF).

Hooded Merganser

Uncommon tv, rare sr. Saranac River March 21, 1964 (HD) to Schroon Lake December 2, 1973 (JB). Occasional in winter. Max. 35 Heart Bay January 11, 1997 (DLC).

Red-breasted Merganser

Uncommon tv, occasional in winter. Port Henry October 2, 1983 (JDB) to hen Bulwagga Bay May 15, 1994 (GL, JP, SP, HW). Pair Four Brothers May 17, 1975 (JP, PT); hen May 26, 1986 (NB, RBB, JP); newly-hatched chicks June 12, 1998 (JP *et al.*); two drakes June 17,

1989 (NB, GL, JP), two drakes, nine hens June 19, 1989 (NB, JP, SP).
Banded at Four Brothers June 25, 1957; nesting June 3, 1958, another
banded same date found dead August 1960 (*fide* JP). Max. 15
Willsboro Point May 2, 1995 (MG).

Common Merganser
Fairly common sr and wv. Max. 1,000 Westport January 4, 1986 (EJ,
JP).

Ruddy Duck
Pair Keene April 2, 1998 (RWM); two Westport October 20, 1976
(EAM, JP); Ti October 20, 1998 (Mary Thill); female Port Kent
November 3, 1955 (specimen SUNY); three Westport November 3,
1979 (PT); hen Westport November 23, 1997 (TM, SO, JP, DTS) and
November 24, 1997 (WB, RWM).

Osprey
Uncommon tv, rare sr. Webb Royce Swamp March 28, 1998 (MG)
to Saranac River May 23, 1970 (MK); E'town August 26, 1977 (GC) to
Port Henry October 23, 1946 (GC); Schroon Lake November 16, 1973
(JB). Westport December 2 and 24, 1976 (HR, PT); Bulwagga Bay
December 17, 1982 (GF); Coll Bay December 2, 1997 (JGT, PHT).
Max. 15 Coot Hill April 27, 1984 (EJ, JP), May 4, 1988 (EJ), and April
24, 1993 (EJ).

Bald Eagle
Erratic visitor at all times of the year, increasingly regular wv along
Lake Champlain. Bred many years ago at Blue Ledge; also near Split
Rock Point where there are recent sightings. Northbound migrants
Coot Hill March 24, 1990 (MAM) to Crown Point May 24, 1996 (DN,
JP). Max. 12 Westport March 13, 1998 (four ad., eight imm. — JP,
PHT); 10 Ti – Westport January 25, 1995 (Amtrak "Adirondack" crew)
and 10 Port Henry – Wickham Marsh January 11, 1997 (NYS
Waterfowl Count).

Northern Harrier
Rare sr. Westport March 9, 1976 (PT) to Wadhams November 26,
1996 (JGT, PHT); occasional in winter. Fall arrival Ray Brook August
26, 1974 (JK). Max. 12 Whallonsburg April 10, 1994 (DTS).

Sharp-shinned Hawk
Fairly common tv, rare sr, occasional in winter. Max. 34 Coot Hill
April 28, 1992 (EJ).

Cooper's Hawk
Very rare sr. Essex March 26, 1976 (JP) to Crown Point October 26,
1974 (HiPkAu); migrating north Moriah May 15, 1980 (GC); Saranac
Lake December 28, 1974 (RH); Blue Ridge Road January 2, 1975 (TB);
E'town-Wadhams Rd. January 15, 1987 (David Keefer); Chapel Pond
January 25, 1981 (BC).

Northern Goshawk
Formerly rare, now fairly common sr in forest around 2,000';
occasional in winter. Max. five Owl Pate Pond September 25, 1985
(MB); breeding adult arrived Paradox February 21, 1983 (MB); tv Coot
Hill May 4, 1988 (EJ).

Red-shouldered Hawk
Rare sr in lowlands. Crown Point March 20, 1987 (JDB) to E'town
November 26, 1973 (GC); Wadhams c. December 16, 1977 (Teresa A.
Fitz-Gerald) and Whallonsburg January 2, 1978 (BE, DN) — same
bird?

Broad-winged Hawk
Fairly common sr. Chapel Pond March 15, 1977 (Paul Bishop); one
Wadhams March 30, 1975 (WP, Sherry Stapell) and Coot Hill April 9,
1989 (EJ) to Saranac Lake October 15, 1986 (DB, MKB) and Westport
December 15, 1979 (Margaret Harris, Peg Rood). Dark morph Coot
Hill April 24, 1993 (EJ). Max. 183 Coot Hill April 28, 1992 (EJ).

Swainson's Hawk
Dark phase migrating north Witherbee June 10, 1997 (GC).

Red-tailed Hawk
Uncommon sr, especially in wilder second growth areas in the 3,000'
range, fairly common tv. Regular in winter. Western dark morph imm.
Westport February 28, 1998 (Wally Koenig, John Kolodziej, JP). Max.
125 Coot Hill April 15, 1994 (EJ).

Rough-legged Hawk
Fairly common wv. Coot Hill October 4, 1982 (JDB) to Essex May
16, 1982 (CS) and into late May (GR). Max. 13 Crown Point

December 17, 1974 (TB, TNM).

Golden Eagle
Rare tv, very rare sv; has bred. Coot Hill April 4, 1988 (EJ) to Coot Hill May 9, 1989 (EJ); Goodnow Mt. October 2, 1991 (WC) to Wadhams December 24, 1994 (BE, DN) and December 25, 1996 (MG); Westport January 25, 1995 (DTS); Split Rock February 22, 1997 (JP, DTS). Max. three Northwoods Club November 10, 1994 (Lloyd Stotz).

American Kestrel
Fairly common sr, a few in winter. Max. 16 Middle Road, Essex August 8, 1981 (GC).

Merlin
Formerly rare tv, reported from Mt. Skylight July 1905 (EE) and North Elba July 22, 1926 (AAS), but no evidence of breeding. Young bird barely capable of sustained flight Cascade Mt. summer 1985 (Frank Nicolletti); active nest Lake Placid August 4, 1993 (Glen & Sue Cameron). Now a rare sr and tv with two Lake Placid nests by 1995 (seven fledged — TD, LM) and 1996 nestings in Lake Placid (three fledged — LM) and Saranac Lake (two fledged — RH); two young hand-reared and released Ray Brook August 15, 1997 (NS). Transients E'town March 19, 1974 (GC) to Saranac Lake May 22, 1992 (DB, MKB); Westport August 4, 1977 (blue adult — JP, GBR) to Westport January 19, 1975 (JP, PT).

Peregrine Falcon
Formerly common sr, nesting as late as 1955 at Four Brothers (TL) and Pitchoff Mt., E'town (WRS), when extirpated as nester by DDT. Hacked near latter eyrie 1981-1983 (DEC); pair Westport cliff July 27-August 5, 1984 (GF, EJ, JP *et al.*) and first nestings in 30 years Keene and Wilmington 1985 (DEC). Now an uncommon sr and tv with eight active eyries fledging a total 14-15 young in 1998 (DEC); latest Willsboro eyrie November 18, 1996 (JP) and nearby Reber November 30, 1996 (DN); pair at this eyrie overwintered 1998-99 (Amtrak "Adirondack" crew), through March 18, 1999 (J.C. Cribbs, JP).

F. p. tundrius. Three Coot Hill April 25-28, 1989 (EJ); North Hudson October 8, 1978 (GR — specimen to Cornell U.). Many transients undoubtedly pertain to this race.

Gyrfalcon
White morph, Wadhams January 20, 1994 (Anne LaBastille).

Gray morphs, E'town November 19, 1993 (JP); Essex December 18-19, 1993 (RWM, JP); Whallonsburg December 19, 1992 (TB, RH); Lewis December 21, 1991 (TB, JP); Moriah March 1, 1982 (GC); Coot Hill April 27, 1982 (EJ).

Dark morphs, Essex November 23-December 8, 1995 (DTS); Newcomb November 29, 1977 (AC, WC); Moriah January 10, 1982 (DLC); Ti February 19, 1982 (DLC).

Gray Partridge
Six Westport January 23, 1981 (Gary Will) were the remnant of a November 1988 covey of 14, following Red-tailed Hawk predation.

Ring-necked Pheasant
Uncommon pr in eastern Essex County.

Ruffed Grouse
Common pr.

Spruce Grouse
Upper AuSable Swamp (EE); male Chubb River about 1940 (Harold H. Axtell); Cold Brook, St. Armand (recent *fide* GTC); Elk Lake June 26, 1968 (FRS); slopes of Phelps Mountain December 1, 1972 (TB); Bloomingdale Bog winter 1976 (GTC) and photo taken in summer (Ed Worthington); seen and heard drumming Chubb River April 24, 1980 (Francine & Paul Buckley); male Elk Lake Road August 12, 1984 (John Bull); male Blue Ridge Road early October 1984 (TNM, DS); Tahawus trailhead late June 1990 (Evelyn Greene).

Wild Turkey
Hen Moriah May 2, 1976 (*fide* TNM); breeding Essex July 1977 (*HiPkAu Newsletter* 5:52), now a fairly common pr. Max. 65 Westport April 4, 1999 (Joseph Gentles).

Northern Bobwhite
Willsboro August 6-9, 1893 (collected — AGP), now extirpated. A bird calling Ti June 5-10, 1997 (GDC) was undoubtedly an escape.

King Rail
Saranac River December 31, 1967 (RH, DY).

Virginia Rail
   Rare sr. Webb Royce Swamp May 1, 1997 (RWM, NS) to Webb
Royce Swamp August 6, 1997 (NO, Marilyn C. Smith).

Sora
   Rare sr. North Elba 1930's (GC); Ray Pond June 9, 1972 (GC);
Essex Station June 11, 1977 (GC). Confirmed breeder (Atlas). Essex
Station May 11, 1977 (EAM, JP) to Wells Hill Road, Jay October 22,
1973 (RH).

Common Moorhen
   Six pair breeding at Ti marsh in 1930's (GC); several pair still present
in 1970's (GC, BM, JM); two June 25, 1989 (TH); Ray Brook Marsh
June 7, 1997 (TD); adults with young Webb Royce Swamp July 30,
1989 (JPa, NP) and July 11, 1992 (TM, JP); several heard at Wickham
Marsh August 29, 1975 (Suzanne Case, KM). Essex May 6, 1954
(MM) to Ti October 14, 1935 (GC).

American Coot
   Very rare tv. Westport April 9, 1999 (WW) to Newcomb April 15,
1971 (*fide* PM); Webb Royce Swamp October 5, 1986 (RB, JP) to
Westport November 24, 1974 (PT). Five winter records. Max. 12
Crown Point October 25, 1989 (GF).

Black-bellied Plover
   Rare tv. Westport May 21, 1980 (GC) to Moody Pond May 24, 1992
(DB, MKB); Westport August 17, 1975 (GC) to Westport November 5,
1978 (DG, JP). Max. 21 Four Brothers October 27, 1985 (RBB, TM,
JP).

American Golden-Plover
   Usually rare tv. Willsboro August 19, 1969 (HD, GM) to Newcomb
November 2, 1993 (Andrew Saunders). An estimated 200-300 were in
a winter wheat field at Essex between August 29 and September 14,
1974 (JP and many others).

Semipalmated Plover
   Rare tv. Ti May 17, 1980 (EJ, JP, DT, JET) to Bulwagga Bay May
19, 1991 (EJ); Westport July 30, 1983 (GC, JP) to Westport October 2,
1946 (GC). Max. five Westport August 29, 1979 (JP) and Westport
August 27, 1993 (William E. Krueger, Charles W. Mitchell).

Piping Plover
Westport August 26, 1993 (RH) to August 28, 1993 (JP, DTS *et al.*)

Killdeer
Fairly common sr, common tv. Essex March 1, 1975 (GBR, CS) and
Westport March 1, 1998 (AR) to Westport December 13, 1973 (JP).
Max. 100 Essex September 4, 1974 (JP).

Greater Yellowlegs
Uncommon tv. Essex April 21, 1975 (JP) to North Hudson May 29,
1971 (JP); Willsboro July 21, 1995 (Mouth Boquet River — MG) to
Westport November 7, 1988 (GC). Max. four Crown Point April 30,
1980 (GC).

Lesser Yellowlegs
Rare tv. Bloomingdale April 10, 1990 (RH) to Westport May 21,
1995 (RWM, MAB); Webb Royce Swamp July 10, 1993 (JBB, TM) to
Westport October 7, 1970 (GC).

Solitary Sandpiper
Fairly common tv. Essex April 26, 1974 (JP) to May 30 (EE); Clear
Pond July 6, 1905 (H. Achilles) to Ti October 14, 1935 (GC). Max.
eight on one pond, Essex August 2, 1974 (JP).

Willet
Keene Valley July 7, 1982 (GC, Evan & Ives Hannay, EJ) to July 9,
1982 (BE); Paradox August 4, 1976 (J. Mahay); Westport August 18,
1975 (JP, DG, KM, PT).

Spotted Sandpiper
Fairly common sr, found nesting as high as 3,000' Scott Pond July 13,
1980 (JP). Essex April 30, 1967 (FW) to Westport October 29, 1979
(GC); in a plowed field at Essex December 19, 1998 (RWM, Brian
McAllister).

Upland Sandpiper
Rare tv and very rare sr. Keene April 26, 1978 (photographed —
Ralph D. Geiser and WAC) to Wadhams September 3, 1975 (JP, GBR,
CS); bred Essex 1970 (DW). Confirmed breeder Ti (Atlas). Max.
seven Essex August 26-27, 1978 (DN).

Whimbrel
Four Willsboro spring 1969 (DW); three Willsboro late July 1964 (Mrs. W. Tero).

Ruddy Turnstone
Rare tv. Four Brothers May 21, 1982 (JP *et al.*) to Four Brothers June 16, 1978 (JP); Westport August 2.1977 (EAM, JP) to Westport October 3, 1985 (GC). Max. seven Four Brothers August 19, 1994 (RWM).

Red Knot
Westport August 30, 1977 (GC, EAM, JP, CS) and the same distinctively marked individual at Port Henry August 31 (GC); Westport August 27-29, 1979 (GC, JP).

Sanderling
Rare tv. Westport July 25, 1977 (GC) to Four Brothers September 19, 1983 (TB, GF, JP) and September 19, 1986 (RBB, JP), mouth of Boquet River same day. Max. 6 Westport to Bulwagga Bay September 2, 1976 (GC, D. Cate, DN).

Semipalmated Sandpiper
Rare tv. May 18 (EE) and Ti May 18, 1995 (DR) to four Essex Station May 19, 1980 (EJ, JP); Westport July 8, 1995 (JP, SP, RW) to Westport October 2, 1946 (GC). Max. 22 Westport July 30, 1977 (JP).

Western Sandpiper
Westport May 15, 1987 (EJ); four fall records, Westport August 8, 1987 (GC) to Westport August 27, 1980 (GC, Janet Carroll, JP).

Least Sandpiper
Uncommon tv, even occurs on waters at higher elevations with floating vegetation (TM). Crown Point May 9, 1935 (GC) to Four Brothers June 9, 1990 (JBB, GL, JP); Westport July 8, 1995 (JP, SP, RW) to Westport September 20, 1975 (JP, PT). Max. 15 Four Brothers May 26, 1986 (NB, JP) and Westport May 15, 1987 (EJ, JP).

White-rumped Sandpiper
Very rare tv. Westport August 24, 1975 (GC) to Bulwagga Bay November 1, 1978 (JP). Max. c. 15 Bulwagga Bay October 21, 1978 (JP, DT, JET).

Baird's Sandpiper
Very rare tv. Westport August 19, 1979 (EJ, JP) to Westport
September 26, 1975 (GC, TNM) and Essex October 29, 1937 (GC).
Max. four Westport September 7, 1979 (JP, GC).

Pectoral Sandpiper
Uncommon tv. Four Brothers May 26, 1986 (NB, JP) to Four
Brothers June 9, 1990 (JBB, GL, JP); Westport July 15, 1991 (GC, JP)
to Westport November 7, 1988 (GC). Max. 25 in storm Lake Placid
October 9, 1976 (DN); max. five Westport November 1, 1988 (GC).

Purple Sandpiper
Whallonsburg March 29, 1978 (on highway — Lester Sweatt, PS).

Dunlin
Ti May 18, 1985 (DR) to Bulwagga Bay May 22, 1982 (Richard
Marrus, JP); Bulwagga Bay September 29, 1982 (GC) to Bulwagga Bay
November 1, 1978 (JP); Westport November 30, 1974 (GC, TB, TNM,
JP, CW). Max. 40 Newcomb May 20, 1978 (WC *et al.*); fall max. nine
Westport October 24, 1989 (GC).

Stilt Sandpiper
Westport August 29, 1987 (GC, EJ, JP); Saranac Lake September 15,
1996 (TD).

Buff-breasted Sandpiper
Essex September 8, 1974 (EBM, JP).

Short-billed Dowitcher
Very rare tv. Near Four Brothers May 9, 1977 (EAM, JP); 15 flying
north Lake Flower May 26, 1968 (RH); Westport July 30, 1977 (GC,
TNM) to Westport August 28, 1979 (TC, GR).

Long-billed Dowitcher
Westport August 6, 1991 (GC, JP); Westport September 25-October
18, 1983 (TB, GC, RH, EJ, TNM, JP).

Common Snipe
Fairly common tv, local in summer. Ti April 7, 1976 (BM) to Saranac
River November 5, 1949 (Philip Weidel). Distraction display Lake
Placid June 11, 1982 (GC, GR); transients Westport August 17, 1988
(EJ) to September 8, 1987 (GC). Max. 12 Bloomingdale October 20,

1972 (Raymond DeVore).

American Woodcock
Fairly common sr. Keene Valley March 9, 1976 (D. Parsons) to
Elizabethtown November 11, 1979 (JP).

Wilson's Phalarope
Westport July 29, 1980 (GC, JP).

Red-necked Phalarope
Clear Pond August 12-14, 1951 (FRS); Westport August 24-27, 1975
(GC, JP, PT); North West Bay October 4, 1980 and two near Split
Rock Point October 5, 1980 (DY); Westport October 28, 1982 (TD).

Red Phalarope
Mid-lake from Port Kent ferry June 13, 1981 (Peter Zita); Westport
November 21, 1984 (GC, TNM).

Parasitic Jaeger
Port Henry September 12, 1970 (Stephen Everett); in a plowed field
at Essex September 15, 1979 after Hurricane Frederic (GBR, CS, JP,
PT, WP); imm. dark morph on open lake Westport November 1, 1997
(Liz Lackey, Theodore Murin, Lisa Osborne) to November 8, 1997
(RWM); a juv. dark morph jaeger (sp.) there December 7-8, 1997
(Theodore Murin) was quite possibly the same bird; imm. dark morph
Westport January 16, 1999 (JP, DTS, RW).

Long-tailed Jaeger
Four miles south of Four Brothers June 7, 1977 (Dr. George LaBar).

Laughing Gull
Imm. Crown Point early August 1993 (WS *et al.*) to August 5, 1993
(TH).

Franklin's Gull
Westport July 11, 1984 (GC, EJ).

Little Gull
Rare tv. Crown Point May 25, 1996 (GH, JP); Westport August 29,
1980 (GC, JP) and August 29, 1987 (GC) to Westport January 3, 1978
(two adults — GC, TNM). Max. three adults Crown Point October 25,
1986 (photographed — WE, RBL, NLM, Christopher Rimmer).

Black-headed Gull
  Adult open lake Port Henry October 29, 1988 (WE, RBL, NLM).

Bonaparte's Gull
  Common, but erratic tv. Westport June 25, 1989 (TH) and Four
Brothers June 27, 1989 (MAM) through January when Lake open; one
in a field outside Lake Placid May 28, 1983 (LM), two Auger Lake July
25, 1996 and one August 2, 1994 (GH), unusual inland. Port Henry
April 6, 1997 (TB, RWM, JP) and Westport the same day (TB, JP) to
Westport May 21-31, 1986 (GC). Max. 750 Westport November 28,
1979 (GC).

Ring-billed Gull
  Abundant throughout the year along shores of Lake Champlain,
frequenting plowed fields as far as E'town. Has bred on Four Brothers
since 1949 (VT Fish & Game Dept.); 13,583 nests May 16, 1998
(RWM); 500 Lake Placid dump June 29, 1975 (Genesee Ornithological
Society).

Herring Gull
  Fairly common throughout the year along the shores of Lake
Champlain. About 141 pairs bred in 1998 on Four Brothers (JP).
Formerly bred Elk Lake (EE) and Wolf Pond, Newcomb 1934 (CEJ).

Thayer's Gull
  Second-year bird Lake Flower March 26-April 1, 1996 (TD —
pending NYSARC approval).

Iceland Gull
  Lake Placid May 28-31, 1975 (at dump — MW, JP); Four Brothers
June 21-23, 1979 (*L.g. kumlieni* — JP, DT); Four Brothers July 3, 1977
(*L.g. kumlieni* — JP, GBR, CS, photographed by EAM); Westport
October 28, 1996 (JP, SP, DTS); Willsboro Point November 3, 1973
(GC); Lake Placid November 9, 1987 (RG); Lake Placid November 24,
1990 (at dump — RH); two Lake Placid November 25, 1989 (Mirror
Lake and dump — RH, LM); Lake Flower November 25-December 4,
1995 (RH); Westport January 5, 1986 (GC); two Essex January 19,
1983 (EJ, JP); Westport February 14, 1989 (GC).

Lesser Black-backed Gull
  Port Henry June 7, 1984 (GC, TB, TNM); Lake Placid November 7,
1987 (Mirror Lake — RG); adult, Westport December 9, 1980 (EJ, JP).

Glaucous Gull

Two Lake Placid November 25, 1987 (Mirror Lake and dump — RH, LM); Saranac Lake dump December 12, 1984 (RH); Westport December 16, 1995 (Laurel Carroll, TD) to December 17, 1995 (RW); Westport December 17, 1977 (WS, PT); Westport December 20, 1997 (JP *et al.*); Lewis dump December 27, 1997 (JAC); Westport January 4, 1997 (RWM, JP, DTS); Whallon's Bay January 25, 1989 (CL, RL).

Great Black-backed Gull

Uncommon wv, occasional in summer. Bred Four Brothers since 1975 (Mrs. Carl Buchheister); 10 pairs June 10, 1995 (JP); Lake Placid dump June 27, 1980 (JP, Tim Stiles) and November 25, 1989 (RH, LM). Max. 165 Westport December 16, 1995 (Ferrisburg CBC).

Sabine's Gull

Port Henry October 26, 1980 (GC); juvenile Crown Point October 29, 1988 (WE, RBL, NLM).

Caspian Tern

Crown Point May 9-10, 1992 (GH, JP); Bulwagga Bay May 15, 1974 (GC, TNM); Four Brothers June 3, 1989 (Timothy L. Barnett, JP); Port Henry June 13, 1984 (GC, Julia Hammond); Auger Pond July 20, 1998 (GH).

Common Tern

Rare sv into September off Split Rock Point (JPa). Two floating on a piece of driftwood, Essex, on the remarkable date of March 30, 1975 (EBM).

Forster's Tern

Two Crown Point April 14, 1994 (Dwight Cargill, TH, Judith Peterson).

Sooty Tern

Lake Champlain September 6, 1876 (Merriam, *Auk* 1:59); it is interesting that one occurred at Rutland, Vermont, the same day (*Birds of Vermont*, Robert N. Spear, Jr., Compiler, Burlington:Green Mountain Audubon Society, 1976, p. 68).

Black Tern
  Uncommon sv. Ti May 7, 1977 (BM, JM) to Split Rock Point into
September (JPa). Present at Ti marsh to June 22, 1975 (max. six —
BM, JM, GC) and June 28, 1976 (GC). Possible breeder Ti (Atlas), but
no recent records.

Thick-billed Murre
  Port Henry December 11, 1950 (collected — TL), one of a small
flight in northeastern New York.

Black Guillemot
  Westport January 7-10, 1978 (photographed — Hudson Mohawk
Bird Club, GC, JP).

Rock Dove
  Fairly common pr. Max. 265 Whallonsburg September 30, 1979
(GBR, CS).

Mourning Dove
  Fairly common pr, as high up as Averyville in winter (GC, LM) and
Trudeau March 10, 1976 (EA).

Passenger Pigeon
  Extinct. Huge numbers Crown Point, 1749; nested, bones found
(*HiPkAu Newsletter* 7:24: *Peter Kalm's Travels in North America*,
Adam B. Benson, ed., NY: Wilson-Erickson, 1937, p. 252 and 369).
Specimen Willsboro October 9, 1891 (AGP).

Black-billed Cuckoo
  Uncommon sr. E'town May 10, 1935 (GC) and Crown Point May 13,
1998 (JP) to Whallonsburg October 8, 1979 (GBR, CS).

Yellow-billed Cuckoo
  Very rare sr. Moriah May 13, 1975 (TB) to Ray Brook September
12, 1964 (JK). Specimen Lake Placid July 1, 1942 (A.H. Benton,
Kingbird 1:59).

Barn Owl
  Westport (*fide* AG); Whallonsburg December 14, 1974 (JP); pair
Northway milepost 113 May 12, 1983 (Ethel Kozma, RM); Essex April
9, 1999 (JP, JGT, PHT) and April 20, 1999 (*fide* Jeff Sherman).

Eastern Screech-Owl

Rare pr in lowlands. Specimen from Willsboro (gray phase — AGP); banded Essex September 12, 1977 (gray phase — JP); photographed Essex December 24, 1977 (red phase — EAM); found dead Willsboro January 6, 1981 (gray phase — *fide* EG); Keene, alt. 1,500' August 17-18, 1994 (red phase — JGT, PHT).

Great Horned Owl

Rare pr as high up as Underwood (GC).

Snowy Owl

Rare, irregular wv. Whallon's Bay October 19, 1978 (JPa) to Spruce Hill April 28, 1992 (Steve Gagnon).

Northern Hawk Owl

Keene February 9, 1982 (BC) to March 20, 1982 (BC *et al.*), but apparently present late December 1981; North Elba November 18, 1992 (WB, RH, CL, RWL) to April 4, 1993 (RH).

Barred Owl

Uncommon pr as high up as Chubb River (TB) and Blueberry Cobble, alt. 2,000' May 29, 1977 (J. and D. Chapman).

Great Gray Owl

Newcomb November 29, 1993 (DTS); Ray Brook December 30, 1983 (DC, JAC, RH, LM); The Glen, Jay December 31, 1978 (*fide* Patricia D. Randorf); Willsboro January 28, 1978 (BB, RBB, IB) and about then (James Wade); E'town January 29-February 12, 1991 (Kurtenbach feeder); Keene Valley February 9-10, 1994 (Runyan feeder); Moody Pond, Saranac Lake March 5, 1978 (*NCCC Bark Eater* 2:4),

Long-eared Owl

Very rare tv and pr as high up as Lake Placid February 1952 (GTC) and December 27, 1998 (LM, Mary Beth Warburton) and Saranac Lake January 5, 1999 (RH). Probable breeder Westport (Atlas).

Short-eared Owl

Crown Point April 7-12, 1975 (TB, Kathryn Collins, TNM); Essex April 14, 1996 (MJK, DTS). Lake Placid November 6, 1987 (RG); Essex December 21, 1996 (CS) to July 19, 1997 (JP, DTS); two

Wadhams December 23, 1989 (E'town CBC); and Essex January 7-10, 1981 (GC, TNM, photographed — JP). Probable breeder Westport (Atlas). Max. four Essex April 21, 1997 (DTS, TS).

Boreal Owl
North Elba mid-December 1896 (Ezra Cornell, Jr.).

Northern Saw-whet Owl
Rare pr. Five young Elk Lake, Upper AuSable Lake, August 3, 1963 (GC, FRS); bred Keene (in Bull 1974, p. 342); young at Augur Lake, E'town and Essex in 1977 (*HiPkAu Newsletter* 5:49) and Newcomb 1989 (TM).

Common Nighthawk
Rare sr. Recorded at Underwood in the 1930's; now regular at Ti and Port Henry; Jay June 27, 1973 (in *Kingbird* 1973). Newcomb April 25, 1983 (Sharon Bissell) to Lake Flower September 23, 1969 (JK).

Whip-poor-will
Fairly common sr; rare in highlands (TM). New Russia March 30, 1991 (SI) and Witherbee April 25, 1985 (CW) to Moriah September 27, 1974 (TB, TNM).

Chimney Swift
Common sr. Coot Hill April 21, 1979 (HiPkAu) to Ray Brook September 4, 1967 (JK) and September 18 (EE). Max. 21 Ray Brook August 15, 1969 (JK).

Ruby-throated Hummingbird
Fairly common sr. Wadhams May 7, 1996 (DTS) to Westport first week of October 1982 (M. & G. Reese).

Rufous Hummingbird
E'town September 3, 1980 (GC, EJ, JP) to September 13, 1980 (JP *et al. — HiPkAu Newsletter* 8:55-6; also *Kingbird* 31:2-3); accepted by NYSARC as *Selasphorus*, sp.

Belted Kingfisher
Common sr, a few in winter. Max. 10 Saranac River September 8, 1973 (TM).

Red-headed Woodpecker
Rare tv. Bloomingdale May 10, 1981 (RH) to The Glen May 26, 1984 (RH); Trudeau September 18, 1965 (EA, HD) to Ray Brook November 1, 1968 (MK); Essex January 28 to late March 1983 (Sally Johnson); pair Essex May 12, 1980 (CS). Adult with young near Westport 1936 (GC); pair at same location 1975 (RB and many others); nest hole there May 14, 1977 (GR). Summer records at Wadhams 1974 and E'town 1975 (JP, PT). Probable breeder (Atlas).

Red-bellied Woodpecker
Ti late January 1984 (AO) to summer 1984 (DLC); Essex August 31, 1990 (CS, Laura Slatkin).

Yellow-bellied Sapsucker
Common sr Moriah March 20, 1974 (AG, TNM) and Bloomingdale March 28, 1998 (TD) to Newcomb November 4, 1971 (PM).

Downy Woodpecker
Common pr.

Hairy Woodpecker
Fairly common pr.

Three-toed Woodpecker
Rare pr, decreasing since Eaton's time. Prefers smaller live and dying balsams and spruce trees in thick stands on mountain slopes or in high altitude swamps. Mt. Marcy 1930's (Robert Darrow); Johns Brook Trail altitude 2,500' July 1937 (Vincent Shainin); Plateau Leanto August 9, 1962 (TB). Bred Copperas Pond 1936, seen there 1947 (AK). Sand Pond recent (*fide* GTC). Chubb River early 1960's June (Guy Tudor); pair there July 27, 1977 (Ken Berlin) and December 24-26, 1977 (LM, GBR, CS). Hurricane Mt. November 3, 1973 (DF, PT). Yard Mt. November 11, 1973 (TM). Lake Colden – Flowed Lands June 27, 1981 (JP, Timothy Stiles); Adirondak Loj April 11, 1998 (MAB, RWM). Vagrants at Westport January 2, 1971 (MLS) and Essex January 13, 1975 (JP, TB, GC); Crown Point September 23, 1981 (JDB).

Black-backed Woodpecker
Uncommon pr. Prefers blowdown and lumbered areas in coniferous forests, also high altitude swamps. Southernmost summer record in county Aiden Lair June 19, 1968 (GC). Vagrants at Crown Point May (TNM); two females Willsboro Point September 21, 1982 (RM); and

Essex October 24, 1974 (JP).

Northern Flicker
Common sr. Ti March 27, 1976 (BM, JM) to North Elba November 14, 1969 (GC). Several winter records.

Yellow-shafted x Red-shafted intergrade Crown Point May 9, 1993 (banded and photographed — JP).

Pileated Woodpecker
Uncommon pr. Max. 13 E'town CBC December 27, 1997.

Olive-sided Flycatcher
Fairly common sr. Paradox May 10, 1993 (MB) to Port Henry September 18, 1981 (John Bruce). Tv Moriah May 31, 1983 (GC).

Eastern Wood-Pewee
Fairly common sr. Moriah May 10, 1990 (EJ) to Saranac Lake September 30, 1967 (RH).

Yellow-bellied Flycatcher
Fairly common sr from about 2,000' to 4,000'. Moose Mt. Pond May 15, 1985 (MKB) to Ray Brook September 10, 1964 (JK). Tv banded Crown Point May 20-21, 1996 and May 24, 1995 (JP). Tv arrived E'town July 30, 1994 (heard — JP); downslope transient Porter Mt. August 8, 1994 (banded — WL).

Alder Flycatcher
Fairly common sr. Ti May 8, 1989 (DLC) and Crown Point May 10, 1993 (banded as "Traill's" — JP) to Butternut Pond August 15, 1932 (singing — GC), Paradox August 19, 1988 (with fledglings — MB), and Corner Pond Brook, Newcomb August 21, 1934 (CEJ); "Traill's" E'town September 18, 1986 (banded — JP).

Willow Flycatcher
Essex Station June 1983 (CS); Essex Station and Ray Brook June 1, 1995 (TD); nest with eggs Essex June 3, 1995 (RWM, DTS); Crown Point June 4, 1984 (GC, AP); Wadhams June 5, 1984 (GC); Lake Placid June 11, 1988 (John Askildsen). Essex Station August 1995 (RWM, JP, SP, DTS).

Least Flycatcher
Common sr. Coot Hill April 29, 1991 (EJ) to Essex September 5, 1979 (banded — CS) and Jay September 16, 1996 (PO).
Eastern Phoebe
Common sr. Crown Point February 22, 1981 (JDB) to Trudeau October 24, 1969 (EA); Ray Brook October 24, 1996 (TD); and Essex November 17, 1976 (JP).

Great Crested Flycatcher
Common sr. Moriah May 1, 1990 (GC) and Coot Hill same day (EJ) to Paradox September 17, 1992 (MB).

Eastern Kingbird
Common sr. Willsboro May 2, 1995 (MG) to Trudeau September 24, 1968 (HD). Max. 14 Crown Point May 11, 1996 (JGT, PHT).

Northern Shrike
Uncommon wv. E'town October 21, 1995 (JP) to Essex April 18, 1996 (DTS).

Loggerhead Shrike
Formerly rare tv, absent in recent years. Westport March 13, 1978 (PT) and St. Armand April 3, 1976 (pair — RH) to Crown Point May 14, 1983 (TB, GC, JP, DR); North Elba July 30, 1925 (AAS) to E'town September 11, 1959 (GC). Bred Essex 1962 (GC) and Westport 1977 (Richard G. and Jeffrey Sherman). Last migrant Mineville April 17, 1991 (GF).

White-eyed Vireo
Singing male Ray Brook May 25, 1996 (TD); E'town October 2-11, 1976 (GC — *Kingbird* 27:28).

Blue-headed Vireo
Fairly common sr. Paradox April 15, 1987 (MB) to E'town October 21, 1981 (banded — JP). Max. seven E'town October 1, 1991 (banded — JP).

Yellow-throated Vireo
Rare sr. May 5, 1936 to August 29, 1935 and September 28, 1978 (all Westport — GC). E'town September 5, 1983 (GC).

Warbling Vireo
Uncommon sr, mostly in villages. Port Henry April 29, 1991 (GC) to Westport September 16, 1946 (GC). Tv on Cobble Hill, E'town May 21, 1969 (GC).

Philadelphia Vireo
Rare tv. Saranac Lake May 6, 1976 (RH) and Crown Point May 11, 1988 (JP) to Westport May 30, 1974 (GC); E'town August 16, 1961 (GC) to Essex October 8, 1978 (banded — CS). Nest June 19 and 20, 1963 (MS, RS) and 1975 (MW, JP), both at Marcy Dam. Other summer records include:

> Near Heart Lake July 12, 1926 (AAS); three July 7, 1932 (GC); July 6, 1933 (GC).
> North Fork Boquet River, Dix Range, not near Lewis as in Bull 1974, three July 3, 1926 (Mr. and Mrs. Philip Livingston & Edward Weyl).
> Upper Cascade Lake June 19, 1954 (W.C. Dilger).
> South Fork Boquet River, Route 73 June 14, 1966 (RH).
> Newcomb July 12, 1978 (GC).
> Spotted Mt. June 11, 1983 (1,350' — DT).
> Elk Lake June 25, 1989 (TH).
> Tahawus June 1, 1994 (2 banded — WL).

All summer records have been in medium height deciduous second growth. Max. three singing males Sanford Lake May 29, 1994 (Frank B. Gill, WL).

Red-eyed Vireo
Abundant sr. Moriah May 10, 1981 (GC) to E'town October 25, 1968 (GC).

Gray Jay
Rare pr. Elk Lake July 1936 (Albert Brand, Jr.); Mt. Marcy 1949 (RSt) and March 1992 (Mike Devlin); Upper Ausable Lake 1964 (Mrs. David Prince); Cold River (MK); Chubb River (Ned Boyajian), adult and young July 6, 1965 (GC); summit of Allen Mt. September 25, 1976 (David Joor); Panther Gorge, alt. 3,000' early June 1979 (TC); Ray Brook July 24-August 2, 1979 (Gene Hilty, WP); Boreas Ponds summer 1984 (AC, WC); vagrant Paradox February 9, 1995 (*fide* MB).

Blue Jay
Abundant sr, some present in winter. Secretive in June. Max. 385 E'town CBC December 27, 1981.

Black-billed Magpie
  Gooley Club May 23-26, 1996 (photographed — Craig and Heidi Plumley, Crystal Tucker).
American Crow
  Abundant sr, irregularly common in winter. Max. 561 E'town CBC December 26, 1992. A 1983 survey found winter roosts near Keeseville, Lake Placid, Wadhams, and Witherbee.

Fish Crow
  Seen and heard Saranac Lake April 7, 1994 (RH).

Common Raven
  Fairly common pr since 1968, following extirpation as a nester during the 19th century. Mt. Marcy October 23, 1875 (EE). Max. 75-150 in paired display flights Rattlesnake Mt. – Mt. Discovery September 27, 1992 (JP, Denise White, HW).

Horned Lark
  Fairly common wv. Heart Lake Road October 29, 1980 (EJ, JP) to Westport April 10, 1997 (TB). Max. 300 Whallon's Bay Road March 17, 1976 (DN).

  E.a. praticola, uncommon sr. Westport February 18, 1991 (BE, DN) to E'town October 4, 1932 (GC).

Purple Martin
  Uncommon sr. Port Henry April 14, 1976 (GC) to E'town September 9, 1964 (GC). Max. 35 Westport August 7, 1976 (GC).

Tree Swallow
  Common sr. Essex March 4, 1974 (JP) to Coot Hill October 17, 1979 (KM, JP).

Northern Rough-winged Swallow
  Uncommon sr. Westport April 23, 1994 (JP, DTS) to Ti July 10, 1932 (GC). Max. 100 Lewis July 30, 1995 (TD).

Bank Swallow
  Common sr. April 21 (EE) to Westport September 16, 1975 (JP).

Barn Swallow
  Abundant sr. E'town April 9, 1977 (KM, PT) to September 23 (EE).

Cliff Swallow
Fairly common sr. Lewis April 22, 1976 (DN) to September 16 (EE).
Max. 1,000 Lake Placid August 19, 1940 (in Bull 1974).
Black-capped Chickadee
Abundant pr. Max. 974 E'town CBC December 24, 1988.

Boreal Chickadee
Fairly common pr in balsam forests from 1800' to above 4,000'.
Occasional wv and tv at lower elevations. E'town October 8, 1935
(GC) to New Russia through April 1976 (at feeder — PT); one returned
to a Newcomb feeder November 6, 1986 for the sixth consecutive
winter (WC). Two Crown Point May 13, 1982 (one banded — GF,
JP); flock Willsboro Point May 18, 1982 (JP). Max. 23 Chubb River
February 12, 1983 (David Harrison).

Gregory Furness

Boreal Chickadee
Crown Point May 13, 1982

Tufted Titmouse
Very rare visitant and pr in lowlands. First seen at Moriah October

1973 (AG) and Westport May 23, 1974 (GC). Probable breeder (Atlas); fledgling banded E'town August 2, 1998 (JP). Chubb River August 26, 1979 (WP). Max. nine E'town December 1993 (French feeder).

Red-breasted Nuthatch
Fairly common pr. Max. 179 E'town CBC December 23, 1978.

White-breasted Nuthatch
Fairly common pr. Max. 73 E'town CBC December 27, 1980.

Brown Creeper
Uncommon pr. Max. 19 E'town CBC December 27, 1980 and December 26, 1982.

Carolina Wren
Very rare visitor since 1952. Essex August 13, 1965 (MM) and Westport September 2, 1996 (TD) to Essex May 24, 1954 (MM); four 1974 occurrences from Westport about November 6 (RB) to E'town December 26 (RL). Pair at nest with young Port Henry May 16, 1981 (GC, EJ, JP) where a singing male had been present since April; E'town July 3, 1989 (GC). Additional records from Crown Point, Grog Harbor, Moriah, and Saranac Lake fall between October and May.

House Wren
Fairly common sr. Moriah April 20, 1977 (TNM) to E'town October 6, 1980 (banded — JP).

Winter Wren
Fairly common sr, a few in winter. Tv arrived Keene April 4, 1974 (GR) and Essex September 10, 1979 (banded — CS).

Sedge Wren
Willsboro April 30, 1891 (Alvah H.B. Jordan, AGP); summer 1935 at Trudeau, North Elba, Street Road, and in a dry alfalfa field at Westport (all GC). North Meadow June 16, 1994 (banded — WL); pair Essex Station July 23, 1995 (MG)-August 1995 (RWM, JP, SP, DTS). Wadhams September 3, 1975 (DG).

Marsh Wren
Rare sr. Webb Royce Swamp April 20, 1997 (DTS) to Crown Point September 30, 1931 (GC).

Golden-crowned Kinglet
Fairly common pr. Max. 58 E'town CBC December 27, 1986.

Ruby-crowned Kinglet
Common tv, rare sr mainly in the highlands. Paradox March 26, 1981 (MB) and E'town April 5, 1981 (banded — JP) to Ray Brook November 16, 1966 (JK). Tv E'town May 20, 1977 (GC). One wintered at feeder Moriah 1975 (AG); two Westport December 19, 1998 (TM, JGT, PHT, RW).

Blue-gray Gnatcatcher
Rare tv and sr since 1974, when there were four records in May. Essex April 22, 1975 (JP) to E'town September 17, 1986 (RBB). First nests at Schuyler Is. May 29, 1976 (DG, JP, PT) and at Crown Point May 13, 1977 (EAM, JP).

Robert C. Wei

Blue-gray Gnatcatcher at nest
Crown Point May 1995

Northern Wheatear
Bobsled Run Road September 28-29, 1984 (CL, RWL, RH *et al.*).

Eastern Bluebird
Fairly common sr. Occasional in winter. Max. 25 Westport January 1995 (AR).

Veery
   Common sr. Split Rock Point April 25, 1995 (MG) to E'town September 26, 1976 (GC).

Gray-cheeked Thrush
   Very rare tv. Willsboro May 12, 1889 (specimen — AGP) to Crown Point May 23, 1993 (banded — JP); Keene Valley September 11, 1991 (banded — WL) to Moriah October 13, 1990 (GC). Spring transients Moriah May 19-20, 1985 and May 22, 1984 (both GC); fall transients E'town September 26, 1991, September 30, 1993, and October 1, 1991 (all banded — JP).

Bicknell's Thrush
   Uncommon sr from timberline on Mt. Marcy down to 3,400', exceptionally 2,750' at Lake Colden; see also *Aubudon Field Notes*, October 1953. Elk Lake May 31, 1983 (MS, RS) and Flowed Land June 6, 1981 (JP) to Porter Mt. October 24, 1994 (banded — WL). Tv arrived E'town September 29, 1994 (banded — JP). Max. six Whiteface Mt. September 26, 1948 (GM).

Swainson's Thrush
   Common sr from about 2,000' to 3,000', rarely lower. Moriah May 8, 1983 (TB) to Westport October 26, 1974 (HiPkAu). Split Rock Point December 20, 1975 (DG, JP, PT). Tv Port Henry May 25, 1981 (GC); tv E'town village August 29, 1980 (GC).

Hermit Thrush
   Common sr. Ti April 7, 1988 (GDC, Malinda Chapman) and Chilson April 7, 1991 (DR) to Newcomb November 5, 1971 or '72 (PM). Two Moriah December 1, 1979 (CW); Saranac Lake feeder December 4-29, 1989 (RH); Ray Brook January 8-12, 1963 (JK).

Wood Thrush
   Fairly common sr. E'town April 30, 1936 (Ednah Hubbard) to E'town October 13, 1974 (GC).

American Robin
   Abundant sr, a few in winter.

European Starling
   Common pr in towns and around farms. Max. 400 Crown Point October 23, 1982 (GC).

Gray Catbird

Common sr. Saranac Lake April 30, 1994 (RH) to Ray Brook
October 21, 1966 (JK), Saranac Lake November 13, 1976 (RH),
Bloomingdale Road November 23 through December 1975 (RH, LM);
Moriah December 6, 1998 (TM, SO, JP); Westport January 1971 (RB).

Northern Mockingbird

Rare visitor since 1960, now a rare pr breeding. Crown Point April
14, 1980 (GC) to E'town November 16, 1967 (GC); three records at Ti
from December 7, 1975 (BM, JM) to April 1966 (JC); Ti winter 1982;
Essex December 16, 1995 (JP, RW) and Westport the same day (MJK,
DTS). Nest with eggs Crown Point May 17, 1980 (EJ, JP, DT, JT);
pair with young Crown Point June 30, 1979 (GC, DT).

Brown Thrasher

Uncommon sr. Moriah April 14, 1980 (MV) to Ray Brook November
9, 1966 (JK); Bloomingdale Road December 19, 1971 (RH); Lake
Placid January 2, 1982 (EJ, JP); E'town January 17-24, 1975 (RWL,
GC); E'town February 10, 1990 (SP).

American Pipit

Rare spring, fairly common fall tv. Bloomingdale April 11, 1990 (RH)
to Ray Brook May 19, 1966 (JK); summit of Whiteface Mt. beginning
September early 1960's (GC), summit of Cascade Mt. September 13,
1964 (GC), summit of Mt. Skylight September 15, 1994 (JGT, PHT),
summit of East Dix September 27, 1995 (Dave Russell), and summit of
Rocky Peak Ridge October 6, 1992 (WL) to Crown Point November 7,
1993 (DTS). Max. 200 Essex November 11, 1979 (GBR, CS).

Bohemian Waxwing

Very rare, irregular wv. Westport November 4, 1995 (MJK, DTS) to

Bohemian Waxwing – Elizabethtown November 7, 1995   *John M.C. Peterson*

Coot Hill April 27, 1993 (EJ); has appeared in all but two winters since 1979-80. Max. 450 Keeseville-Port Douglas January 11, 1987 (TM, JP) and 672 Essex-Westport December 16, 1995 (TD, RWM, JP *et al.*).

Cedar Waxwing

Common sr, erratic in winter; common 1974-75. Max. 155 Westport March 13, 1998 (JP, JGT, PHT) and 442 Essex-Westport December 15, 1984 (GC, RH, EJ, JP).

Blue-winged Warbler

Crown Point May 9-10, 1981 (JP *et al.*); Crown Point May 18, 1998 (GH, JP, SP).

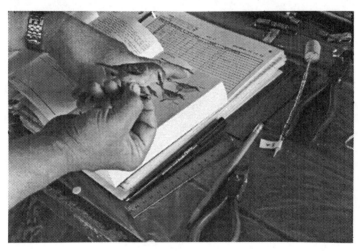

Gordon E. Howard

Blue-winged Warbler
Crown Point May 18, 1998

Golden-winged Warbler

Witherbee May 11, 1985 (CW); Crown Point May 15, 1985 (banded — JP); Hadley Pond May 20, 1978 (JP, WP); two males Willsboro May 21, 1983 (DN); Chesterfield May 29, 1983 (DC, JAC); several June records; several years Essex (JPa) and Paradox (MB); Willsboro July 24, 1998 (Matt Medlar); E'town August 29, 1964 (GC); E'town September 6, 1976 (GC); Ausable Forks October 17, 1988 (struck window — George Doyle). Probable breeder (Atlas). Max. three singing males Crown Point May 12, 1991 (JP *et al.*).

Lawrence's Warbler
North Hudson (Atlas Survey — Robert Kirker).

Tennessee Warbler
Uncommon spring, fairly common fall tv. Crown Point May 11, 1980 (EJ, JP) and May 11, 1985 (TB) and Paradox the same day (MB) to Moriah June 6, 1984 (GC); E'town August 4, 1979 (banded — JP) to E'town October 8, 1976 (GC) and Moriah November 4, 1979 (TNM). Bred North Elba 1926 (AAS). Other summer records include:

> Indian Falls, alt. 3,700' (AAS); July 13-16, 1949 (several birds — RSt).
> Hurricane Mt., about 2,000', July 10, 1930 (singing male — GC and Laidlaw Williams).
> Pair Wilmington Mt., about 3,000', June 4-10, 1966 (RH, DY).
> Pair South Fork Boquet River, alt. 1,900', June 26, 1970 (GC).

All summer records have been in high deciduous second growth. Banded E'town July 21, 1979 (female — JP) and July 22, 1979 (male — JP), alt. 700'. Max. 25 Moriah May 24, 1983 (TB).

Orange-crowned Warbler
Very rare tv. Round Top April 28, 1996 (JGT, PHT) and Ray Brook May 11, 1968 (singing — MK) to Four Brothers May 23, 1987 (JP, WP, *et al.*); E'town September 15, 1981 (EJ, JP) to Wilmington October 13, 1972 (GC).

Nashville Warbler
Fairly common sr. Chilson April 29, 1991 (DR) and E'town April 29, 1995 (MG) to St. Armand November 8, 1975 (*fide* LM). Tv Whallonsburg August 16, 1977 (banded — CS).

Northern Parula
Rare tv. Ray Brook April 30, 1968 (JK) and Paradox May 7, 1984 (MB) to E'town May 28, 1935 (GC); E'town August 31, 1933 (GC) to Ray Brook October 14, 1966 (JK). Rare sr in swampy woods at about 2,000'; has decreased.

Yellow Warbler
Fairly common sr. Saranac Lake April 30, 1994 (RH) to September 1 (EE).

Chestnut-sided Warbler
Common sr. Coot Hill May 2, 1990 (EJ) to E'town September 26, 1974 (GC).

Magnolia Warbler
Fairly common sr. Chilson April 26, 1991 (DR) to Wickham Marsh October 8, 1990 (LRS). Tv Moriah June 4, 1984 (GC).

Cape May Warbler
Uncommon tv. Crown Point May 8, 1976 (DN) to E'town May 30, 1974 (GC) and Essex the same day (JP); Whallonsburg August 11, 1977 (JP, GBR) to Saranac Lake October 10, 1979 (RH). Bred at North Elba 1947 (*Auk* 65:607); seen at Chubb River June 5, 1976 (Urner Club); mouth of Panther Gorge, early June 1979 (TC). A bird appeared at a suet feeder at Moriah December 8-11, 1974 (AG, TB, GC, TNM) and November 1975 (AG); Essex December 11, 1974 (JP). Max. five E'town May 20, 1978 (GC).

Black-throated Blue Warbler
Fairly common sr. Keene April 18, 1996 (RWM, MAB) and April 30 (EE) to E'town October 15, 1972.

Yellow-rumped Warbler
Fairly common sr to timberline; occasional in winter near Lake Champlain. Arrival Moriah April 1, 1990 (GC). Tv Crown Point May 26, 1996 (banded — JP) and Four Brothers August 31, 1986 (TM, JP). Max. 173 banded Crown Point May 12, 1996 (GH, JP, RW).

Black-throated Green Warbler
Fairly common sr Paradox April 26, 1992 (MB) and E'town April 26, 1994 (JP) to E'town October 25, 1937 (GC) and Ray Brook November 10, 1966 (JK). Tv Moriah June 3, 1984 (GC).

Blackburnian Warbler
Fairly common sr. Paradox April 29, 1990 (MB) to E'town October 4, 1974 (GC).

Yellow-throated Warbler
Crown Point May 14, 1995 (Suzannah Dwyer, GL).

Pine Warbler
Rare sr. Port Douglas April 14, 1954 (TL — specimen SUNY) to

Ray Brook October 17, 1966 (JK). Tv Moriah September 22, 1987
(GC). One winter record at Ti feeder (AO). Max. c. 100 North
Country Com. College pond, Saranac Lake October 2, 1997 (TD).

Prairie Warbler

Very rare tv. Coot Hill April 27, 1988 (EJ) to Crown Point May 16,
1988 (banded — JP); Ti August 12, 1962 (JC). A small colony was
discovered at Port Douglas in 1955 (Richard A. Herbert, WRS); two
singing males were there June 21, 1963 (GC). Pair Paleface June 3 to
June 27, 1983 (GC, EJ, JP, AP).

Palm Warbler

Rare tv. Crown Point May 8, 1976 (DN) to Lewis May 20, 1935
(GC); Ray Brook August 31, 1966 (JK) to Saranac Lake October 27,
1979 (RH). Max. 12 Crown Point May 8, 1986 (JP).

> *D. p. hypochrysea.* Port Douglas April 11, 1954 (TL —
> specimen SUNY) to Crown Point May 12, 1998 (J.C. and
> Susan Cribbs, J.R. Cribbs, GH, JP); Wadhams September 3,
> 1975 (JP, GBR, CS) to E'town October 25, 1979 (banded —
> JP) and Wadhams October 31, 1994 (DTS).

Bay-breasted Warbler

Fairly common tv. Moriah May 10, 1981 (GC) to E'town June 1,
1974 (GC); E'town August 6, 1979 (JP) to E'town September 28, 1970
(GC). Uncommon sr in balsam woods.

Blackpoll Warbler

Uncommon spring, common fall tv. Moriah May 11, 1975 (MV) to
E'town June 4, 1926 (GC); E'town August 21, 1973 (GC) to E'town
October 11, 1932 (GC). Fairly common sr from 2,900' (Mt. Jo — GC)

Blackpoll Warbler – Crown Point May 1997   *John M.C. Peterson*

to timberline, but occurs as low as 1,000' near Johnson Pond, 1,720' along Boreas River, 2,000' at Preston Ponds, and 2,366 at Marcy Dam in summer (JP *et al.*).

Cerulean Warbler

Keene Valley May 14, 1994 (LS, ASt); singing male E'town May 30, 1998 (heard only – MG); singing male, Moriah June 11, 1983 (TB, GC, TNM); Jay September 12, 1992 (Anne Sherman, LS, ASt).

Black-and-white Warbler

Fairly common sr, E'town April 22, 1976 (GC) to Ray Brook October 6, 1961 (JK). Westport December 17, 1974, record (killed striking window, eaten by cat – AG, in *Kingbird* 25: 107-108) not recognized (*contra.* Bull 1998, p. 481).

American Redstart

Fairly common sr Port Henry May 3, 1984 (MaryAnne Allen, CW) to Moody Pond October 23, 1981 (DB, MKB). Essex November 10, 1975 (J. Peter Martin, JP) and Essex November 18, 1979 (CS).

Prothonotary Warbler

Saranac Lake May 6, 1983 (Karen Miller).

Worm-eating Warbler

E'town May 10, 1979 (banded — JP, seen by DT, PT); Wadhams May 11-12, 1993 (DTS).

Ovenbird

Abundant sr. Moriah April 29, 1984 (TNM) and Paradox April 29, 1990 (MB) to Hurricane Mt. October 10, 1997 (JGT, PHT). One at Dickerson feeder Westport December 21-24, 1974 (GC, Freda Howard, TNM).

Northern Waterthrush

Uncommon sr. Auger Lake April 21, 1980 (song well-described — DC, JAC) to Westport October 1, 1970 (GC). Tv Moriah May 28, 1983 (GC); apparent tv banded E'town July 21, 1979 (JP).

Louisiana Waterthrush

Rare sr on rushing lowland brooks to as high as Paradox and Berrymill Pond (MB). Moriah April 21, 1998 (TB) to Ti August 1, 1950 (GC). Three singing males Hammond and Hoisington Brooks, Westport May 27, 1984 (EJ, JP). Nest with five eggs Moriah May 29,

1993, hatched June 11 (TB).

Kentucky Warbler
Singing male seen at close range, E'town May 17-18, 1969 (GC).

Connecticut Warbler
Wadhams May 18, 1995 (DTS) to Crown Point May 20, 1996 (DM, JP); Crown Point August 21, 1996 (Judy & Roger Heintz); Nun-da-ga-o Ridge August 31, 1996 (JGT, PHT); E'town September 10, 1983 (EJ, KO, JP); adult male E'town September 24, 1977 (GC).

Mourning Warbler
Uncommon sr as high as 3,900' (Big Slide Mt. — GC). Crown Point May 14, 1988 (banded — JP) to E'town September 14, 1962 (GC) and Saranac Lake October 4, 1987 (RH). Tv Moriah June 5, 1983 (GC).

Common Yellowthroat
Common sr. Chubb River April 29, 1995 (LO, PO) to E'town October 24, 1979 (GC). Moriah December 18, 1973 (Helen Phinney); Westport December 26, 1992 (TH, DTS).

Wilson's Warbler
Uncommon tv. Crown Point May 11, 1985 (banded — JP) to Ti June 6, 1971 (JC); Saranac Lake August 13, 1983 (RH); E'town August 21, 1967 (GC) to Ray Brook October 3, 1966 (JK). Pair, nest, and three eggs North Elba July 1, 1978 (DN, JP — *Kingbird* 28:215-220); pair same location June 7, 1980 (JP, DT, JET, PT). Max. three Four Brothers May 23, 1987 (JP, WP *et al.*).

Wilson's Warbler – Crown Point May 1995   *Robert C. Wei*

Canada Warbler
Fairly common sr. Essex May 7, 1979 (CS) to Paradox September 27, 1990 (MB). Unusual after early September. Tv Moriah June 7, 1984 (GC); tv E'town August 13, 1994 (banded — JP).

Yellow-breasted Chat
Crown Point May 1954 (Lucien Lambert); Ti May 24, 1990 (DLC); Ti May 25, 1957 (JC); Wadhams mid-July 1983 (DTS); Newcomb Lake summer 1988 in alders (TB).

Summer Tanager
Changing male singing, E'town May 30, 1976 (GC — *Kingbird* 26:150).

Scarlet Tanager
Uncommon sr. Paradox May 3, 1993 (MB) to Saranac Lake October 14, 1990 (RH) and Street Road October 28, 1969 (JC).

Eastern Towhee
Uncommon sr as high as 2,700' (old burn, Spotted Mt.). Occasional in winter. Saranac Lake April 4, 1968 (RH) to Saranac Lake October 30, 1992 (RH).

American Tree Sparrow
Abundant wv. E'town October 16, 1972 (GC) to Essex May 14, 1974 (JP) and Crown Point May 24, 1997 (DTS, TS).

Chipping Sparrow
Abundant sr. Moriah Center March 24, 1991 (GF) to Trudeau December 28, 1950 (GM). Three Saranac Lake December 31, 1976 into February 1977 (RH). Max. 110 E'town village October 3, 1977 (GC). Flocks have departed by October 20.

Clay-colored Sparrow
Singing males seen Crown Point May 11, 1985 (GH, JP), May 22, 1996 (banded — DN, JP, RW), and June 2-10, 1995 (John Ciaccio, MG, RWM, JP, DTS); Willsboro June 18-July 14, 1980 (GC, EJ, JP); Upper Jay June 19, 1974 (Bruce McP. Beehler); Lake Placid June 24-25, 1963 (AK, EA, HD); Wilmington June 28-29, 1963 (AK); and Whallonsburg June 29, 1978 (DN, JP). Saranac Lake October 24-29, 1976 (RH).

Field Sparrow
Fairly common sr. Essex March 26, 1977 (EAM, JP) to Essex November 11, 1972 and December 25, 1974 (both JP); three Westport December 26, 1983 (GBR, CS); Wadhams December 29, 1995 (DTS); two E'town January 1981 (DT, JET).

Vesper Sparrow
Fairly common sr. Essex March 22, 1997 (TM, SO, JP) to Saranac Lake November 3, 1965 (RH). Tv E'town village September 23, 1977 (GC). Westport December 15, 1979 (GC).

Lark Sparrow
South Meadow September 8, 1981 (Daniel O'Keeffe, KO, JP).

Savannah Sparrow
Abundant sr. Wadhams March 22, 1976 (banded — JP, GC) to three Essex November 28, 1996 (DN — one darker race) and E'town November 30, 1975 (GC). Tv Four Brothers May 22, 1987 (JP, WP *et al.*); tv E'town August 12, 1981 (banded — JP, Peter Rock); tv E'town village September 3, 1982 (GC). Max. 45 Whallonsburg October 4, 1979 (banded — CS).

Grasshopper Sparrow
Crown Point May 20, 1997 (GL, JP); Ray Brook August 4, 1995 (TD) to Westport August 25, 1976 (GC, TNM).

Nelson's Sharp-tailed Sparrow
Westport October 23-24, 1983 (TB, GC, RH, TNM, JP, DR).

Fox Sparrow
Uncommon tv. Moriah March 23, 1974 (AG, TNM) to Auger Lake May 7, 1986 (GH). E'town October 1, 1978 (JP *et al.*) to Elizabethtown November 15, 1995 (MG); occasional in winter. Max. 25 Ray Brook October 25, 1963 (JK).

Song Sparrow
Common sr occasional in winter. Arrived Severance March 20, 1974 (Mildred Tyrrell). Max. 30 Whallonsburg October 16, 1979 (banded — CS).

Lincoln's Sparrow
Uncommon tv. Essex May 4, 1975 (two banded — DF, JP, PT) and

Coot Hill May 4, 1990 (EJ) to Crown Point May 24, 1993 and May 24, 1996 (banded — JP); E'town August 30, 1972 (GC) to E'town October 20, 1975 (GC). Uncommon sr in boggy areas around 2,000'. Max. eight Elizabethtown October 7, 1995 (MG).

Swamp Sparrow
Uncommon sr. Essex April 12, 1974 (JP) to Westport October 26, 1975 (GC). Tv Port Henry September 8, 1982 (GC); two Westport November 2, 1983 (TB, GC, TNM); Webb Royce Swamp December 18, 1996 (DTS).

White-throated Sparrow
Abundant sr to high altitudes, occasional in winter.

Harris's Sparrow
Moody Pond October 27-November 5, 1980 (DB, MKB, GC, GTC, RH *et al.*; banded and photographed — JP).

White-crowned Sparrow
Fairly common tv. Schroon Lake April 15, 1974 (JB) to 2,400' on Porter Mt. May 27, 1994 (WL); summit of Mt. Skylight (4,926') September 12, 1998 (JGT, PHT) to Wadhams December 6, 1937 (GC); four midwinter records; Ti February 17, 1984 (JC). Max. 60 Wilmington October 13, 1972 (GC).

Dark-eyed Junco
Abundant sr to timberline; winters in small numbers. Max. 450 E'town village April 24, 1974 (GC).

Lapland Longspur
Rare wv. Summit of Algonquin Peak October 22, 1994 (Candy & John Hess) to Westport March 23, 1974 (TNM) and Essex the same day (JP).

Snow Bunting
Abundant wv. Newcomb October 19, 1978 (WC) to Lake Placid April 10. 1965 (RH). Max. 1,000 Essex January 9, 1985 (GR).

Northern Cardinal
Seen at Wadhams 1933; Crown Point 1935; Essex 1949; Bloomingdale 1961, now a fairly common pr, breeding.

Rose-breasted Grosbeak
Fairly common sr. Heart Bay April 14, 1991 (DLC); Newcomb April 23, 1971 or '72 (*fide* PM) and Bloomingdale April 26, 1968 (Isabel Williams) to E'town October 3, 1973 (GC) and Saranac Lake October 3, 1995 (RH). Max. 10 E'town September 15, 1979 (GC).

Black-headed Grosbeak
E'town May 7, 1989 (BB, IB); Saranac Lake November 20-22, 1987 (photographed — Frank Gauthier, RH).

Blue Grosbeak
Male Port Kent June 17, 1964 (HD — *Kingbird* 14:215-216).

Indigo Bunting
Fairly common sr. Keene April 30, 1983 (Thomas Hale) and Moriah May 1, 1983 (TB, GC, TNM) to E'town October 7, 1975 (GC). Max. five E'town September 17, 1979 (GC).

Dickcissel
Three Trudeau August 25, 1962 (EA, HD); E'town August 27, 1962 (GC); E'town October 20-26, 1975 (GC). Keeseville August 13, 1955 (collected, specimen SUNY Plattsburgh — TL), in *Kingbird* 5:89.

Bobolink
Fairly common sr. Ti April 21, 1956 and April 23, 1957 (both JC) to Essex September 14, 1974 (GC) and Jay September 14, 1996 (LO, PO). Tv E'town May 27, 1980 (GC, JP); tv arrived E'town August 2, 1974 (GC).

Red-winged Blackbird
Abundant sr taking increasingly to fields since 1950. Essex February 21, 1981 (EJ, JP) to Lake Placid December 31, 1967 (RH). Max. 1,000+ Essex March 10, 1977 (EAM, JP).

Eastern Meadowlark
Fairly common sr. Westport February 18, 1991 (BE, DN) to Bloomingdale November 16, 1971 (TM), Saranac Lake November 30, 1974 (RH), Westport December 20, 1980 (GC), and Westport December 31, 1974 (TB, TNM).

Yellow-headed Blackbird
Male Blue Ridge Road December 8, 1980, after storm (DS); imm.

male Westport March 11, 1998 (JGT, PHT); male Keene October 17, 1998 (ST).

Rusty Blackbird
Uncommon tv, Bloomingdale March 17, 1990 (RH) to Lewis May 21, 1935 (GC); E'town September 18, 1968 (GC) to Moriah November 22, 1974 (TB, TNM); Lake Placid December 25, 1980 (BC); Saranac Lake December 31, 1988 and January 1, 1989 (RH, LM); two Wadhams February 19, 1981 (Linda Curtin). Uncommon sr in wet highlands. Max. 275 E'town October 20, 1970 (GC).

Brewer's Blackbird
Saranac Lake October 24, 1990 (RH); Essex December 6-14, 1984 (GC, JPa, JP).

Common Grackle
Fairly common sr arrival Moriah March 6, 1974 (AG); occasional in winter. Max. 400 E'town September 27, 1976 (GC).

Brown-headed Cowbird
Fairly common sr, uncommon in winter. Max. 150 E'town April 8, 1976 (GC).

Orchard Oriole
Very rare tv and sr. Ti May 9, 1976 (BM, JM) and Crown Point the same day (DN, JP) to Essex July 9, 1974 (GBR, CS). Five records in 1975. Confirmed breeder Crown Point and Ti (Atlas).

Baltimore Oriole
Fairly common sr. Ironville April 25, 1991 (DR) to Saranac Lake September 23, 1995 (RH) and Trudeau October 20, 1965 (HD); Keeseville November 28-December 3, 1983 (John Gillen); Moriah December 10-11, 1981 (GC, TNM, CW).

Pine Grosbeak
Fairly common, irregular wv. North Elba October 21, 1972 (RH) to Lewis April 21, 1976 (DN); "a few" Essex May 16, 1982 (CS). Max. 136 E'town CBC December 27, 1981.

Purple Finch
Fairly common sr, irregularly common on migration and in winter. Max. 1,000 Westport December 27, 1976 (EAM, JP, GBR, CS).

House Finch

Seen at Moriah August 16, 1974 (TB, TNM); two Westport December 14, 1974 (TB, TNM); Essex April 4, 1975 (banded — JP, PT); Wadhams July 20-21, 1975 (JP, PT); Willsboro August 17, 1975 (W.A. Richie); Whallonsburg August 8, 1979 (JP), banded August 13 (CS). Breeding confirmed (Atlas). This western species, accidentally introduced into western Long Island in the 1940's, has thrived and spread to many eastern states.

Red Crossbill

Uncommon, irregular pr. Max. 131 Essex – Westport December 20, 1997 (TB, KM, JP *et al.*) and 63 E'town CBC December 27, 1997.

White-winged Crossbill

Rare in summer in northwestern Essex County; uncommon, erratic in winter county-wide. Three Elk Lake June 30, 1975 (Alan Klonick, in Bull 1976, p. 46); pair nest-building Northwoods Club July 15-19, 1958 (Hugh Fosburgh); singing male, Wright-Algonquin Col late July 1980 (Mike Rosenfeld). Nest built Chubb River February 22, 1975 (JP, PT and many others, song recorded — WAC) and December 30,1979 (DN). Max. 200 Lake Placid February 15, 1997 (three singing males Chubb River — Richard Clements).

Common Redpoll

Irregularly abundant wv. North Elba October 26, 1997 (Elle, Grace, and Kathy Brown, WB, RWM, MAB) to Upper Jay May 10, 1998 (MAB) and Newcomb May 11, 1996 (Mary Ward). A big incursion started January 23, 1974 (Moriah, TNM). Max. 300 Schroon Lake March 23 (JB); 470 banded E'town January 12-April 17, 1996 (JP).

Hoary Redpoll

Very rare wv. Essex November 22, 1997 (JP), Lewis December 27, 1986 (at dump — Katherine & Nan Eagleson), and E'town December 29, 1993 (banded and photographed — JP) to E'town April 17, 1996 (two banded — JP). Max. five E'town February 8, 1994 (four banded birds — JP).

Pine Siskin

Erratic, fairly common to abundant pr. Max. 413 E'town CBC December 26, 1987; 403 banded E'town February 22-May 7, 1981 (JP). Green morphs banded E'town March 3, 1990 (three — JP), April 11, 1990 (one — JP), February 16, 1993 (two — JP) and February 5, 1997 (one — JP).

American Goldfinch
Abundant sr uncommon to abundant wv. Max. 364 E'town CBC December 26, 1976; 1,585 banded E'town January 1-April 29, 1993 (JP).

Evening Grosbeak
First in New York State, E'town winter 1875 (Sewall Sylvester Cutting, in Brewer 1875); Elk Lake and Clear Pond July 1942 (Edward Fleisher, C.H. Rogers); in the last 25 years has become a common sr and abundant wv. Max. 1,000 Schroon Lake November 6, 1974 (JB).

House Sparrow
Abundant pr in towns and on farms. Max. 150 at one farm, Crown Point September 26, 1980 (GC).

John M.C. Peterson

Hoary Redpoll, *C. h. exilipes*
Elizabethtown April 9, 1996

ESSEX COUNTY, NEW YORK
Birding Sites

These 21 productive areas offer only a starting point for birders, but over the years have proven themselves by providing a host of county records.

WHERE TO FIND BIRDS

1. **Belfrey Mt.** — Hawk lookout spring and fall. Trail starts about one half mile NW of Witherbee on Belfrey Hill Road; an excellent view for an easy ten minute climb.

2. **Bulwagga Bay** — Lookout point for water birds. When the lake level is low enough, scan the jetty across the bay through a telescope.

3. **Cascade Lakes** — Look and listen for ravens around the cliffs. Route 73 between Keene and Lake Placid.

4. **Chapel Pond** — Scan cliffs. On Route 73 between Route 9 and Keene Valley.

5. **Chubb River** — Coniferous forest. Chance for three-toed woodpeckers. White-winged Crossbills; Rusty Blackbird. Gray Jay is a long shot. About 1½ miles SW of Lake Placid on Averyville Road at bridge. In a few hundred feet keep straight on wood road where Northville-Placid trail bears left.

6. **Coot Hill** — Hawk lookout spring and fall. From Moriah Corners, about two miles W of Port Henry, head S on the S. Moriah Road. After 2.8 miles, turn left (east) on the unpaved Lang Road, follow road right at third farmhouse from the corner, uphill, then left (east) at cemetery to the summit.

7. **Crown Point Peninsula** — A good weather trap in May, on brushy slope SW of Amherst's Fort (W of Lake Champlain bridge). An occasional large owl is turned up in the winter in the coniferous groves at the Campground (S of bridge). Check the narrows around the bridge for waterfowl and gulls.

8. **Elk Lake** — Excellent northwoods at about 2000' altitude. Good for Common Loon, Northern Goshawk, Black-backed Woodpecker, Olive-sided Flycatcher, Ruby-crowned Kinglet, Northern Parula and many other warblers, Rusty Blackbird. From exit 29 of the Northway drive W 5 miles, then turn N on dirt road. The first ten minutes of Dix trail is deep coniferous forest. Best walk is on local trails around SW corner of lake and up Marcy trail or west side of lake (crossover between these trails about a mile to the north).

9. **Essex Harbor** — Good possibilities for waterfowl in mid-winter in pockets of open water. Observe from the ferry dock and Begg's Point Park just south of the Old Dock House.

10. **Essex Station** — A marsh producing Sora and Virginia Rail and Blue-winged Teal, and an occasional shorebird. 1½ miles W of Essex on Route 22. Willow Flycatcher and Sedge Wren may be found south along the RR tracks.

11. **Essex Triangle** — The "Magic Triangle" formed by the Clark, Cross, and Lake Shore Roads around the Webb Royce Swamp (*q.v.*), noted for open-country raptors, American Pipits, Bohemian Waxwings, and sparrows. A "greater" triangle includes the Anger Hill and Whallon's Bay Roads running south and east of Whallonsburg. Good year-round birding.

12. **Four Brothers Is.** — Gulls, cormorants, Gadwall and other ducks, shorebirds, and breeding herons. Off Willsboro Pt. Transportation can sometimes be arranged privately at the Essex or Willsboro Bay Marinas.

13. **Heart Lake** — A variety of northwood species. Turn S off Route 73 about 2½ SE of Lake Placid. Look for Lincoln's Sparrow in boggy spots on way in. Marcy Dam is a two mile hike from Heart Lake; Philadelphia Vireo has occurred below the dam. A climb up Wright or Algonquin Peaks should produce Bicknell's Thrush near timberline, as on other peaks.

14. **Ticonderoga Marsh** — Least Bittern, Common Gallinule, Marsh Wren breed. Black Tern have occurred in May and June. Can be approached on foot from the Fort or by driving a mile SE of town and walking N on the RR tracks.

15. **Upper Ausable Swamp** — Coniferous woods habitat. Black-backed Woodpecker and Gray Jay are possible. A five mile hike from Elk Lake on the Marcy Trail.

16. **Webb Royce Swamp** — Pied-billed Grebe, herons, geese and ducks, raptors, rails, and Marsh Wrens; Bohemian Waxwings may be found in winter. Within the "Magic Triangle" on the west side of the Lake Shore Road between Westport and Whallon's Bay, but best viewed from the Clark Road which runs along the west side of the swamp.

17. **Westport Beach** — Excellent for shorebirds from late July into October, especially if the Lake level is low enough to expose mud flats. Good for waterfowl October to early January; flocks of Bonaparte's Gulls are frequent. Check the public beach in the center of the village and the boat launch site at the north end of the village.

John M.C. Peterson

Scanning North West Bay, Westport

18. **Whiteface Mt.** — Bicknell's Thrush near timberline. The American Pipit has occurred on the bare summit in early September. Migrating hawks have been seen from the Memorial Highway to the summit. Turn N off Route 86 at Wilmington.

19. **Wickham Marsh** — Rails and occasionally ducks, Least Bittern, Marsh Wren. One mile N of Port Kent on Lakeside Road.

20. **Willsboro Point** — Water birds. About 2.7 miles N of the village, W of Farrell Road is a cove of Willsboro Bay; drive in to the N side of it. E of there is a productive bay on Lake Champlain. One can drive to the tip of the Point.

21. **Wilmington Notch** — Cliffs for large birds; Winter Wren. Midway between Wilmington and Lake Placid on Route 86.

BIBLIOGRAPHY

Andrle, Robert F. and Janet R. Carroll, eds. *The Atlas of Breeding Birds in New York State*. Ithaca and London: Cornell University Press, 1988.

Beehler, Bruce McP. *Birdlife of the Adirondack Park*. Glens Falls: Adirondack Mountain Club, 1978.

Bull, John. *Birds of New York State*. Garden City: Doubleday/Natural History Press, 1974.

Bull, John. *Supplement to Birds of New York State*. Cortland: Federation of New York State Bird Clubs, 1976.

Bull, John L. *Bull's Birds of New York State* / Emanuel Levine, editor. Ithaca and London: Cornell University Press, 1998.

Eaton, Elon H. *Birds of New York*. 2 Vols. Albany, New York: Univ. State of New York, 1910, 1914.

field notes (formerly *Audubon Field Notes, American Birds*, and *National Audubon Society FieldNotes*). American Birding Association in alliance with the National Audubon Society.

Johnson, Charles E. "Land Vertebrates of the Huntington Forest." *Roosevelt Wildlife Bulletin* 6:4 part 1. 1937.

Kingbird. Federation of New York State Bird Clubs, Inc.

Peterson, John M.C., ed. *High Peaks Audubon Newsletter*. High Peaks Audubon Society, Inc. Vols. 1-25 (1973-1997).

Saunders, Aretas A. "The summer birds of the northern Adirondack Mountains." *Roosevelt Wildlife Bulletin* 5. 1929.

INDEX

NOTES